ESSAYS ON ROMAN CULTURE

ESSAYS ON ROMAN CULTURE

THE TODD MEMORIAL LECTURES

Edited by A.J. Dunston

SAMUEL STEVENS
HAKKERT & COMPANY
TORONTO & SARASOTA
1976

Printed in The United States of America

International Standard Book Number
0-88866-560-1

Library of Congress Catalogue Card Number
74-84098

A. M. Hakkert Ltd.
554 Spadina Crescent
Toronto, Ontario
M5S 2J9

3807 Bond Place
Sarasota, Florida
33580

CONTENTS

FREDERICK AUGUSTUS TODD

Professor of Latin in the University of Sydney

1922-1944

Frederick Augustus Todd was born in Sydney on 14 March, 1880. Eighteen years later he matriculated from Sydney Public High School and entered the University of Sydney where he graduated in 1901 with First class Honours in Latin and Greek, gaining also a University Medal for Classics. Awarded a Woolley Travelling Scholarship, he studied at the Universities of Leipzig (1901-2) and Jena (1902-3), being awarded by the latter the degree of Ph.D. for his thesis *De Musis in Carminibus Poetarum Romanorum Commemoratis* (Jena, 1903). He returned to Sydney as Assistant Lecturer in Latin, was Assistant Professor from 1913 to 1921 and Professor from 1922 to 1944.

Todd played a full part in University life: he was Dean of the Faculty of Arts and a Fellow of the Senate from 1930 to 1957. He was for several years a member of the Board of the Sydney University Union, and, in 1913-14, its President. For ten years he acted as Secretary of the Extension Board.

Outside the University he served for many years as a member of the New South Wales Board of Examiners and of the Board of Secondary School Studies. He was in 1909 a co-founder of the New South Wales Branch of the Classical Association.

In 1940 his book *Some Ancient Novels* was published by Oxford University Press.

An appreciation of his life and work and a select bibliography was contributed by his distinguished colleague, Professor A. D. Trendall, to the *Union Recorder* of July 13, 1944, pp. 99-100.

Professor Todd died suddenly in June, 1944. His friends, colleagues and former pupils created by subscription a Memorial Lecture Fund which is administered by a Committee on which are representatives of the three bodies to which Todd dedicated his services—the University, the Union and the Classical Association of New South Wales. From time to time, as accumulated interest provides the necessary funds, a distinguished scholar is invited to deliver a lecture. The first seven of the Lectures have previously been printed, but are now issued as a collection, together with the Eighth Lecture, delivered in 1971. Future lectures will, in the first instance, be published as they occur.

Augustus the Patrician

EDWARD TOGO SALMON

It is a rare distinction to be invited to deliver the Todd Memorial Lecture. The prestige of the series is recognized on all the continents, and any student of classical antiquity is bound to feel proud to be associated with the illustrious scholars responsible for its renown. But for me there is a very particular reason for feeling appreciative as well as honoured. I first met the name of the scholar whom we are remembering tonight over fifty years ago, on the very first day that I entered Sydney High School. In those days the school stood in the heart of the district known as Ultimo, and on the second floor of its solid if somewhat grimy building there was a large hall where student assemblies, concerts, and similar funtions were held. Affixed to the walls of that hall were wooden boards, on which were inscribed, in letters of gold, the names of the boys who, over the years, had particularly distinguished themselves at their studies. Prominent among them was the name of F. A. Todd. The man himself I did not meet until some years later, when I came up to this institution, here to discover how abundantly justified was my boyish awe at his scholastic achievements. He had just been promoted to the chair of Latin in succession to T. A. Butler, and the depth of his learning and breadth of his interests, his meticulous accuracy and academic authority won the immediate respect of all whose good fortune it was to sit at his feet. And to respect there was quickly added affection, for to the austerity of the scholar Todd conjoined the generosity of the friend. His concerned interest in those he taught was shown in many ways, but I shall mention only one. After leaving Sydney I went to Cambridge, and, on the day before my final examinations there were to begin, a cable arrived from Todd, to cheer me on and wish me luck. You will understand, Mr. Deputy Chancellor, why tonight I feel very much moved and deeply grateful to the committee that has granted me the privilege of paying what tribute I can to his memory.

The impressive range of Todd's interests meant that there was no difficulty in finding a topic suitable for the present occasion. On the contrary, it presented a veritable embarrassment of riches. A paper on the Hellenistic romances or on the graffiti of Pompeii would have been very appropriate; or something on Cicero, in view of the zest with which Todd expounded the *Verrines* or the *De Oratore* and in view of the Ciceronian elegance of the Latin he himself was wont to compose. But, above all, there was the Golden Age, a source of continuous and abiding pleasure to him, as all those who attended his classes on Horace and Vergil will undoubtedly recall. For that reason some aspect of the emperor after whom Frederick Augustus Todd was named seemed indicated; and the aspect I have chosen is one that I am sure he himself would have found congenial: Augustus the patrician.

Tacitus, Suetonius and Cassius Dio, between them,

describe how Julius Caesar used a special law, the *Lex Cassia* of 45 BC, to create new patricians, including in their number his own great-nephew Octavian, later to become Augustus.[1] His example proved infectious, and Augustus was not long in copying it. Indeed Augustus set to work while still Octavian. He himself could serve as model. Some of his new patricians were created as early as 33,[2] although later, as Augustus, he was careful not to draw attention to this fact, probably because his action in 33 was high-handed and irregular. He did, however, record how he swelled the ranks of the patricians four years later: 'When consul for the fifth time' (that is, in 29 BC) 'I increased the number of patricians, on instructions from the People and the Senate' (*patriciorum numerum auxi consul quintum iussu populi et senatus*: *Res Gest.* 8.1). In 29 he could claim some sort of constitutional authority for his behaviour: he had had a law passed, the *Lex Saenia*, empowering him to create patricians, just as his great-uncle had done with the *Lex Cassia*.[3]

Augustus thus reveals, in part at any rate, what he did; but he nowhere tells why he did it. He remains, as always, enigmatic, something like the sphinx engraved upon his signet ring.[4]

One reason for him to add new members to Rome's oldest aristocracy comes to mind automatically. He wished to bestow honour and distinction upon those of his supporters who had been most active and useful on his behalf. And, in the days before Actium and in the case of men from obscure Italian families that could stand a little glamourizing, this was very probably his principal motive. But most of Augustus' new patricians seem to have been created after Actium, and comparatively few of them were Italians intent upon launching their families into the troubled waters of Roman politics for the first time.[5] Most of his new patricians were members of families from Rome itself, families that were anything but strangers to Roman public life. Nor can they all be proved to have been exceptionally active in promoting the fortunes of Augustus in his early days. Hence it looks as if the wish to requite his more zealous partisans was not Augustus' only reason for enlarging the patriciate. For that matter, his rewards to followers of proved fidelity were usually of a more substantial nature than mere exaltation of rank. He saw to it that they acquired great riches and occupied powerful positions in the Roman state; and, although it is true that at Rome good birth always obtained favour and enjoyed privilege, patrician status was not in itself an inevitable or necessary prerequisite for wealth and power.

It seems likely that Augustus was chiefly influenced by his determination to preserve whatever he found of value in the Roman state. In his earlier days, it must be admitted, he had shown but scant respect for traditional Roman ways: he had been the revolutionary young ruffian of Perusia.[6] But after Actium, when his position was firm and unassailable, he could afford to cultivate political respectability; and the reliefs of the *Ara Pacis Augustae* eloquently advertize his eagerness to be known as the upholder of things Roman, the promoter of Roman traditions, the saviour of venerable Roman practices. After 31 he became the conservative stalwart, the champion of the *mos maiorum*, the one who would preserve and if necessary revive the great institutions of Rome. He himself in his autobiography, if such the *Res Gestae* may be called, insists on his support of, and observance of, Roman usages: 'I refused any office inconsistent with the custom of our ancestors' (*nullum magistratum contra morem maiorum delatum recepi*: 6.1); or again, 'I rescued many customs of our ancestors that in our generation were lapsing into desuetude' (*multa exempla maiorum exolescentia iam ex nostro saeculo reduxi*: 8.5). He repaired old

Roman temples and erected new ones. He revived Roman cults and rituals. He exalted Romans above non-Romans. He frowned on an over-tolerant admission of ex-slaves into the Roman citizen body. He encouraged a high birth-rate for Romans. He pushed forward the bounds of Rome's imperial sway. And he began the transformation of Rome itself into a splendid, monumental capital, worthy of the extended dominion he had bestowed upon it. In sum, after Actium his policy was unvaryingly and quintessentially Roman. He, the young revolutionary from Italian Velitrae,[7] became, in Velleius' words, the *conditor conservatorque Romani nominis,*[8] the great traditionalist, the hidebound conservative, more Roman than the Romans themselves.

One of the old Roman institutions which he particularly esteemed was the patriciate. This is shown by his regard for his own patrician status, dubious though its aspect must have seemed to many of his contemporaries. Julius Caesar's right to create new patricians, authorized by the *Lex Cassia* though it was, must have struck them as an unprecedented usurpation. Be that as it may, Augustus never questioned his own right to the status, not even when it would have suited his political purpose to do so. He realized, for instance, quite early in his career how politically useful it would have been for him to become a plebeian tribune, and at one time he actually toyed with the idea of taking that office.[9] But, as a patrician, he was debarred from it, and he simply could not bring himself to divest himself of that status in order to become tribune. Of course, he managed to solve this particular dilemma by an astute manoeuvre. He simply took all of the plebeian tribune's rights and prerogatives without ever entering upon the plebeian tribune's office. And thus the emperor's Tribunician Power was born, a remarkable device for making him unlike all other men, 'the expression of his supreme authority,' as Tacitus was to call it.[10] But brilliant constitutional improvisation though the Tribunician Power was, it did make something of a mockery of Augustus' claim never to have accepted a position inconsistent with ancestral usage. Who, under the Republic, ever heard of a man wielding the tribune's powers while not himself an actual tribune? Evidently Augustus was willing to risk the charge of unconstitutional behaviour so as to be able to retain the aura surrounding a Roman patrician of which, as a municipal bourgeois from countryside Italy, he stood in awe. His own enrolment in patrician ranks appealed greatly to his vanity.

Augustus always attached great value to outward trappings of distinction. Note, for example, his attitude to the appellation *pater patriae.* This purely honorific title came his way in 2 BC,[11] and it did not bring with it any concrete or measurable addition to the powers that he already possessed. But it did subtly suggest that Augustus stood in the same relation to the whole Roman nation as a *pater familias* did to his own household. Augustus accordingly depicted his being styled *pater patriae* as the crowning achievement, the supreme glory of his career: it occupies the last chapter and forms the splendid climax and grand finale of the *Res Gestae.*

More than mere snobbery was involved. At Rome high birth and high rank counted for much, and he who could claim to be a patrician, just like him who could parade the title *pater patriae*, would enjoy substantial, practical advantages: he would look like an authentic Roman aristocrat, with incalculable enhancement of his personal prestige (*auctoritas*).

To reinforce Augustus' personal predilection for patricians, there was his conviction that the patriciate was worth saving since it was the nucleus from which the Roman nation had sprung. The patricians were an integral part of the Roman state. They stood at the very heart of the Roman community and were inextricably interwoven with its whole history and greatness. As Cassius Dio was later to remark, 'the patricians are regarded as indispensable for the perpetuation of traditional institutions.'[12] The patricians had always been there, so to speak. Some patrician families reckoned themselves older than Rome itself. The Julii Caesares, for instance, claimed descent from the goddess Venus.[13] The Sulpicii Galbae, less modest, paraded an origin from Jupiter himself.[14] The impudence with which such claims were advanced was no doubt matched by the scepticism with which they were received. Nevertheless it is clear enough that, in a status-conscious society like that of the Romans, the patricians ranked inordinately high. They were the group that had controlled the Republic during its first two hundred years, whcn for long they alone had been eligible for political or priestly office and had managed the state apparatus to suit their own desires. Their supremacy, it is true, had come increasingly under challenge, and in 342 BC a law was passed stipulationg that from then on one of the two consuls was always to be a plebeian and that both of them might be;[15] and when this was followed soon afterwards by recognition of the right of the plebeians to share in many of the priesthoods and to legislate in the name of all Roman citizens, patricians and plebeians alike, one might have expected patrician pre-eminence to come to an end. This, however, did not turn out to be the case. By some means or other, the patricians managed to enjoy prerogatives unspecified by any law and to retain great political power. Tradition, the unwritten *mos maiorum*, the conservative force of custom ensured that at Rome favour was always shown to distinguished birth and to men of means. In theory any Roman citizen should have been able to stand for the consulship; in practice only the well born and the well-to-do could win it. Of recent years valuable studies (some of them from the pens of scholars who have been heard as Todd lecturers)[16] have quite properly emphasized how at Rome social status led to political privilege, reluctant though the Romans were to publicize the fact by their legislation. The powers wielded by certain elements in Roman society may have been extra-legal, but they were none the less real. And among the groups thus favoured were the patricians, Rome's ultimate aristocracy. Right down to 172 BC the patricians somehow managed to keep one of the two consulships firmly in their grasp. Election of two plebeian consuls, theoretically possible ever since 342 BC never actually occurred until 172.[17] And even after 172, in fact right down to Julius Caesar's day one hundred and twenty-five years later, it was far more usual for the Roman state to have one patrician and one plebeian as its consuls than to have two plebeians.

In the office of censor, too, throughout the Roman Republic, patricians were equally prominent; indeed, if anything, they were even more to the fore in the censorship than in the consulship.

Only during the years between the Gracchi and the Social War had the patricians suffered really marked eclipse: the forty-three years between 134 and 91 BC were the only period of the Roman Republic when they did not win consulships, and censorships, on a scale out of all proportion to their numbers.[18] Old Etonians have shown a similar tenacity in hanging on to posts in British cabinets. The conclusion is inescapable: patricians enjoyed something more than mere social superiority.

By the late first century BC, however, their end seemed near. By then the remarkable, long-lived institution of the patriciate was quite clearly moribund. For throughout the centuries of the Republic it had never been kept up to strength. Plebeians had occasionally been adopted by patricians, but not very often, and many patrician families had gradually died out without being replaced by the admission of new ones. Of the fifty patrician *gentes*, or clans, existing in he fifth century BC fewer than half, a mere twenty-two, were still surviving in 367; and by 179 they had dwindled still further, to a mere seventeen. By the end of the Republic the seventeen had become only fourteen; and, between them, these fourteen *gentes* contained only some thirty families, whereas the twenty-two *gentes* still extant in 367 had embraced over eighty.[19]

The hereditary patriciate was manifestly doomed unless new families were added to it. Julius Caesar had done something to revive it, but not very much.[20] Augustus therefore decided to improve on his great-uncle's example; and, had he not acted, the grand old caste must soon have passed into oblivion. For the decline of the patrician families of the Republic continued into the days of the Empire. By the time of the emperor Tiberius (AD 14 – 37) only seven of the fourteen patrician *gentes* of the last century BC still survived, and practically all of these seven had disappeared by the time that the Julio-Claudian dynasty came to its end in 68.[21] It was, quite literally, the newly made patrician families that kept the patriciate alive. They might display subservience more than pedigree, but they were patricians, in name anyway.

But in preserving the patriciate Augustus also transformed it: and thereby he ran the risk of incurring the hostility of the proud patricians themselves. For, like aristocrats everywhere, they resented additions to their exclusive ranks. Some of them, it may be suspected, would have preferred extinction to contamination. But Augustus was not to be deterred. He knew that he could not entirely escape ill-will anyway since some of the patricians must have regarded his own insertion into their midst as a pollution. Evidently he calculated that the credit he would win as a new Romulus, preserving what the old Romulus had created,[22] would more than compensate for any resulting hostility from the old patricians; and there was even the chance that the magnetism of his own success would reconcile the recalcitrants. For, in saving the patriciate, he would save much else besides. Had he not enlarged the patrician caste, other Roman practices and traditions would also have had to be abandoned. In particular, he would not have been able to carry through that programme of religious revival which seemed to him so essential for the rehabilitation of Roman society. Without patricians the traditional Roman religion was scarcely viable, and the decline in their numbers was making it difficult, and would soon make it impossible, to find persons properly qualified to perform various acts of cult and ritual.

The *rex sacrorum*, for example, had to be a patrician. Then there were the *Salii*, the two colleges of priests essential for the proper worship of Mars, the god especially dear to Roman hearts: twenty-four reasonably young patrician males were needed to keep the roster of the *Salii* up to strength. Nor does the tale end there. There were also the *flamines*, priests individually dedicated to the worship of some one specific divinity. Not all of them were patricians, but the four important ones, the three so-called *flamines maiores* and the one superintending the cult of the deified Julius Caesar, did necessarily have to be of that rank, and there was some trouble in finding them. The office of *flamen dialis*, for instance, remained vacant from 87 to 11 BC precisely because candidates with the exact qualifications were hard to find.[23] Moreover, at the very moment when patrician families were becoming rarer, the number of *flamines* threatened to get larger. The newly established cult of the deified Julius Caesar had already made one extra patrician *flamen* necessary, and it was not unreasonable for Augustus to foresee, if not positively to hope, that there would soon be another *divus* to care for.

It was not only the state religion that demanded patricians. They were required in other areas of state business as well. The *interrex*, for example, had to be a patrician, and he was an official of whom Augustus was bound to be uncommonly conscious. For Augustus could not have forgotten the year 43, the year when both of the consuls had lost their lives in the fighting around Mutina, *cum cecidit fato consul uterque pari*, as Ovid puts it.[24] Augustus made up his mind to take their place, and he was even prepared, if need be, to seize the now vacant consulship by force of arms. But he preferred to be able to say that he had obtained the office by legitimate process, and therefore he wanted to go through the formality of being elected into it at Rome. Now, as the consuls for 43 were both dead, this election should have been conducted by an *interrex*. At that moment, however, no patrician could be found at Rome to serve as *interrex*, so that Augustus, or Octavian as he then was, was forced to resort to a very irregular procedure for the staging of his so-called election.[25] He was, of course, made consul: his army would have seen to that in any case; but this consulship, illegal to begin with, had now become doubly so, and Augustus was not likely to forget that a shortage of patricians was chiefly to blame.

Another office reserved to patricians, or so it appears, was that of *princeps senatus*. This would present no problem so long as Augustus himself was alive, he having become *princeps senatus* in 28.[26] But there was still the future to think of. The Roman emperor might become an object of worship, but that would not stop him from being mortal; and some day a successor, a patrician successor, for the *princeps senatus* would have to be found.

Some of Augustus' revivals, even if they did not make

new patricians positively imperative, did at least render them desirable. For instance, he brought the *Troia* game back to life and expanded it. This was an exercise in which companies of aristocratic boys carried out a series of complicated manoeuvres on horseback. In implying that the youthful performers were all patricians Cassius Dio is mistaken:[27] even so, it was obviously desirable that a certain proportion of them should be. The same is no less true of the Arval brotherhood and the college of *fetiales*, both of which likewise seem to have been resurrected by Augustus.

Exaggeration, of course, must avoided. After making allowance for all requirements, both those that were inescapably necessary and those that were merely desirable, the total of patricians needed for state purposes, while urgent and serious, was not overwhelming. Furthermore, it was also spasmodic. Only occasionally would it be necessary to appoint a *rex sacrorum*, a *flamen*, an *interrex*, or a *princeps senatus*; and even if the two colleges of *Salii* kept up a steady demand for patricians, there were the dying old patrician families from republican times to help meet it.

According to Cassius Dio,[28] Julius Caesar's new patricians were 'many.' A similar statement is nowhere made about Augustus. Yet Augustus seems to have created far more of them than his great-uncle. Despite Dio's 'many' it cannot be positively demonstrated that Julius Caesar ever made anybody a patrician except Mark Antony and Octavian:[29] a statement elsewhere in Dio[30] that he did the same for Cicero convinces nobody. Yet Augustus can be shown, by allusions in literature, by inscriptions, and by the careers of certain important personages, to have created at least sixteen new patrician families, and the total may well be even higher than that. Agrippa, for instance, is not one of the demonstrable sixteen. Yet it is inconceivable that Agrippa, Augustus' most useful supporter and closest associate, the husband of his daughter and the father of his grandchildren, was not made patrician, seeing that the honour befell others who were neither related to the emperor nor exceptionally distinguished in themselves.

On the whole the evidence suggests that Augustus created more than enough patricians for the priesthoods and other official positions positively needing them; and presumably he had some motive in doing so.

Patronage will be one explanation. Every member of the senatorial order must have been eager to be promoted to the rank, for it not only enabled a man to cut a grand figure, but also brought with it the prospect of rapid preferment. The first step in the *cursus honorum*, or official career, of a Roman senator under the Empire was to serve on one of the four boards that collectively made up the so-called vigintivirate. But it made a difference on which board one served. The three mint-masters (*tresviri monetales*) were the ones with the brightest prospects: they consistently reached the highest posts later; and patricians were invariably mint-masters during their period of service with the vigintivirate. After the vigintivirate the young patrician was ready for the quaestorship, and this he regularly obtained by being appointed to it by the emperor: unlike non-patricians he was not under the necessity of having to canvass fiercely in the Senate and to fight a real election for the office. The quaestorship was followed by either the plebeian tribunate or the aedileship, and as patricians were ineligible for the former they were logically excused from the latter. Thus they proceeded from the quaestorship to the praetorship in a single bound; and as it was the praetorship that opened the way to the very highest appointments in the Empire, a patrician was fully qualified for them some three years ahead of his non-patricin contemporaries and while still a comparatively young man. Thus patrician status, with its promise of greater certainty and greater celerity in attaining the highest posts, was something worth having. Undoubtedly the above pattern took some time to establish itself and become standardized, but it was already clearly discernible under Augustus. He, in fact, was its creator; for it was he who (in 13 BC) made a period of service on the vigintivirate obligatory for all would-be senators and who (in 18 BC) excused the patricians among them from the aedileship.[31]

The privileged position of the patricians was made to order for the exploitative talents of Augustus. He did not content himself with elevating Italian newcomers who deserved particularly well of him, men like Statilius Taurus from Lucania, or Lucius Arruntius from Atina, or, probably, Vipsanius Agrippa from who knows where.[32] The overwhelming majority of his new patricians were not obscure Italians at all. Of the sixteen families that he is known to have brought into the patriciate,[33] a round dozen were celebrated in the annals of the Republic, families such as the Aelii Tuberones, the Appuleii Saturnini, the Junii Silani and, still more illustrious, the Calpurnii Pisones, the Domitii Ahenorbarbi, the Claudii Marcelli and the Sempronii Gracchi. Evidently Augustus was seeking to conciliate and mollify the old republican element in the Senate, compensating them for the indignity of having Italian upstarts thrust upon them. And, as everybody knows, he was successful: he did succeed in placating and soothing the ruffled feelings of the senatorial class.

In fact, it is no exaggeration to say that his creation of new patricians helped him to carry out his cherished plan of unifying Italy. This may seem strange and paradoxical, for the patriciate might well appear an instrument better suited for stratification than for integration. But the grant of patrician status bribed aristocratic Romans into acquiescence with Augustus' policy of promoting Italian *novi homines* into the consulship; and the prospect of patrician status kept Italians happy with Augustus' policy of fostering Roman ways and customs. Needless to say, he was very selective, reserving the grant of patrician status to comparatively few. But aspirations could be kept alive: every senator could hope that the honour might some day come his way. Augustus' practice helped to weld and fuse Romans and Italians into one nation with a community of outlook and singleness of purpose to an extent that had never been achieved before.

Where Augustus led, later emperors followed. When his successors created patricians, it was for motives very like his. Tiberius, it is true, did not raise anyone to the patriciate, so far as we know, and neither did Caligula. But Claudius took the office of censor in AD 43, and used it to enlarge the patriciate, among other other purposes. As with Augustus, one of his motives was to make acceptable to existing senators a policy which many of them found distasteful. Claudius was aiming to bring more natives from the provinces, especially the western provinces, into the Roman Senate; he was even prepared to adlect natives from unurbanized tribal districts,[34] and to class-conscious Roman senators such persons would appear little better than barbarians. Claudius therefore promoted some senators from Italy, and so far as we know only senators from Italy (including Rome), into the patriciate, thus enabling them to retain their feelings of superiority over the newcomers he was proposing to foist upon them.[35]

Vespasian, the next emperor to create patricians, seems to have behaved in an essentially similar way. Assuming the censorhsip in 73, he began to bring still more natives from the provinces, even some from the eastern provinces, into the Senate; and to calm the outraged feelings that this aroused in existing senators, he made some of the latter, including some originating from the western provinces, patricians.[36] This was a momentous step. To make Roman patricians out of native provincials must have contributed greatly to the unification of the Roman Empire, since it would help to prevent a feeling of alienation from spreading among the provincial bourgeoisie.

The patriciate was thus a useful instrument for imperial policy. It is not to be dismissed as an obsolete relic or as an object of antiquarian curiosity. Under Augustus it helped to unite Italy, under his successors it served to knit the Empire together, and throughout it emphasized the hierarchy; and the emperors of Rome, like the dictators of more recent days, were very well aware that gradations of privilege are the best guarantee for an autocrat's ability to control his inferiors. From of old the Romans were past masters in the art of *divide et impera*.[37]

It was an advantage that the system could be kept going indefinitely by means of periodical inductions of more newly created aristocrats. This was just as well, for the new patricians of the Empire resembled the old patricians of the Republic in showing a distressing tendency to die out. To the ills to which flesh is naturally heir were added the deadly effects of imperial jealousy. The murderous inclinations of malevolent emperors like Nero often made patricians their target; a patrician after all was *capax imperii*, nobody more so, as we shall see. As a result, some patrician families, the Junii Silani for example, were quite literally exterminated. Others, however, displayed a tenacious longevity. Calpurnii Pisones were still prominent in Roman public life late in the second century AD,[38] and an Aquillius, descended from a family made patrician by Augustus, was consul, also in the second half of that century.[39]

In any case, the new patrician families, the short-lived ones and the durable ones alike, contributed many high officials to the service of the Roman Empire. Of Augustus' new patricians, P. Silius Nerva had three sons and three grandsons reach the consulship, and C. Asinius Pollio a son and likewise three grandsons. The descendants of T. Statilius Taurus also included consuls among their number.[40] These three families, as it happened, died out fairly quickly, but others could be, and were, created in their place; and as patrician status was naturally reserved for those who best conformed with the imperial system, the new patriciate would inevitably continue to contribute to the pool of administrative manpower available for imperial purposes.

But if the new patricians had merely decorated the social scene and supplied the Roman Empire with a few of its priests and top administrators, they would be little more than a subject of scholarly interest. In fact, they were something more. For the patricians enjoyed a prerogative of the type that has already been mentioned, the unwritten kind. It was not defined by any letter of the law, but it played a significant role in the development of the history of the Emprie. The record of the imperial succession indicates that, for a very long time, only patricians were considered suitable candidates for the office of emperor. This was one of the *arcana imperii* with which Cassius Dio was well acquainted ('emperors belong altogether to the patrician class' is the way he puts it);[41] but it has passed unremarked by most modern writers on the Roman Empire.

During the first seventy-five years of the Empire, it was regarded as unthinkable that anyone should be emperor who could not claim descent, either by birth or by adoption, from the old republican nobility and indeed from a patrician family in that nobility. This unwritten rule helps to explain Agrippa's self-effacement[42] and the relative ease with which Tiberius got rid of even so powerful a figure as Sejanus; and it will also account for Verginius Rufus' refusal to seize the purple in AD 68 when it looked like his for the taking. It also explains why Scribonianus under Claudius, and Piso under Nero should have thought of themselves as credible pretenders, possible substitutes for the reigning princes: both of these rebels were patricians and descendants of the republican nobility. Likewise the reason for Galba's refusal to imitate Verginius Rufus' reluctance in 68 becomes apparent: Galba, too, was a patrician scion of the republican nobility, so that he had no need to hesitate about seizing the purple. And it is to be noted that the successor he selected for himself, M. Piso Licinianus, belonged to the same class.

Disillusion with Galba led to his murder and to the murder of his intended successor, and there does not seem to have been any other patrician with a suitable republican background left to take his place. The Roman world accordingly had to make up its mind to an emperor who was not from the old republican nobility, as indeed Tacitus expressly informs us.[43] That, however, was not to say that the Roman world now had to discard its age-old preference for high birth. It did not need to accept the proposition that the emperor might now be taken from any level of society at all. If there was no patrician from the old republican nobility available, there was at least the possibility of a patrician from the new imperial aristocracy; and this was the rule that came to prevail. Galba was succeeded by Otho, and Otho in his turn by Vitellius; and both Otho and Vitellius were patricians, the former from a family of Etruscan Ferentum, the latter from a family of Nuceria, in all likelihood the Campanian town of that name. Claudius had been the emperor responsible for making both these families patrician.[44]

The new convention that only patricians, that is the new patricians of the Empire, could aspire to the purple had to be ignored, it is true, when *urgentibus imperii fatis* circumstances proved too much for it; and such circumstances arose later in the year 69. That was the dreadful year of the four emperors, and by the first of July Galba and Otho were both dead and the Emprie was languishing under the misrule of Vitellius. The need of a saviour for the Roman world was distressingly evident. It was Italy, the sober, hard-working Italy of imperial literature, that supplied peace and a *princeps* on this occasion, just as it had done on the previous occasion, one hundred years earlier. But it meant the elevation of a non-patrician. Effectively, by mid-year of 69, the choice lay between Vespasian, commander of the army in Judaea, and Licinius Mucianus, governor of the province of Syria. Neither was a patrician, but Vespasian did at least come from a family that had emerged from obscurity in Augustus' reign and that belonged to the heart of Italy, to a district that had been one of the very first to be romanized;[45] unlike Verginius Rufus, Vespasian was not a native of a region that until recently had been reckoned a part of Gaul. Where Mucianus came from nobody knows;[46] presumably it was a place sufficiently outlandish to make him content to play the role of Agrippa to Vespasian's Augustus. His self-abnegation was certainly not due to any love for Vespasian, since the two men had not even been on good terms until the middle of the year 69. It may be suspected, in fact, that Mucianus came from the provinces [47] and realized that, as such, he would not be acceptable as a candidate for empire. Vespasian himself, for that matter, was none too over-confident. He seems to have been nervous that his own non-patrician status might prove fatal to his chances: that will explain why he hesitated so long before permitting a claim to be made on his behalf. Probably it also explains why many Romans to the very end remained loyal to Vitellius, even after that patrician glutton had himself already expressed a strong desire to abdicate.[48] Even after Vespasian had secured military supremacy, he still thought it prudent to stay away from Rome for months on end, to give the Senate time to pronounce him a patrician and to give the People time to get used to thinking of him in his new patrician guise.[49] And, once in Rome, the newly made patrician sought by various devices to enhance the dignity of his family and make it seem more authentically aristocratic: the *Lex de Imperio* that Vespasian evidently felt necessary to justify his seizure of power (but that no previous emperor seems to have needed), the repeated consulships that Vespasian held (usually with his son for a colleague), the office of censor that Vespasian revived and occupied – all of these things amounted to an attempt on his part to raise the prestige of himself and his family.

The second half of 69 was then entirely exceptional, and this accounts for the accession of a non-patrician as emperor on that occasion. At other times, almost to the very end of the second century, the unwritten rule that only patricians could compete for the purple was regularly observed. The Flavian emperors after Vespasian of course conform to it. Titus and Domitian had inherited patrician status from their father, and it is noteworthy that each of them succeeded without any difficulty. Domitian, it is true, did find himself with a rebellion on his hands half way through his reign; but it is noteworthy that the pretender was himself a patrician, Lucius Saturninus, from a family that may have been elevated to that status ahead of the Flavian.[50]

After Domitian's murder in September of 96, the situation was ominously similar to that after the death of Nero, but another year of four emperors was avoided when the Senate found an elderly patrician upon whom to confer the imperial power. Nerva came from an Italian family that had emerged from obscurity in triumviral days and had been made patrician by Augustus. It is difficult to see what other qualifications he possessed for the exalted role that was now thrust upon him. He had, it seems, helped Nero to suppress the conspiracy of Piso, but otherwise he had had no scintillating career in the service of the Empire. So far as is known, he had held no military or high admininstrative post apart from the consulship, which in any case by his day was little more than a ceremonial sinecure. Like many other senators, Nerva had been content to serve in the urban magistracies and then remain in Rome, passing his life in ways more or less traditional for members of his class. But, unlike most of his fellows, he was a patrician and by that very fact a fit candidate for empire.[51]

Cassius Dio asserts that in 97 Nerva passed over relatives of his own in order to select Trajan as his successor,[52] and modern scholars argue that this inaugurated the system of succession by adoption which gave the Roman world excellent emperors and good government for the next three quarters of a century and more, in fact right down to the day when Marcus Aurelius substituted hereditary for adoptive succession, ensuring the accession of his own son, the worthless Commodus, to the throne of the Caesars in 180. The thesis that succession by adoption was the deliberate and conscious policy of the so-called Antonine emperors is far from convincing.[53] Admittedly Nerva did proclaim the adoption of Trajan, but there is evidence to suggest that the choice may have been forced upon him;[54] and, even if it was not, one must still ask why Trajan should have been the one to be selected. The usual explanation is that he was an experienced soldier and, perhaps more important, that he was at that moment in command of the army of Upper Germany, the nearest to Rome of the really formidable provincial forces. But

Trajan was not the only eminent person available. There was also Licinius Sura, for example. Sura, however, was not a patrician and, presumably because of this, was content to push the fortunes of Trajan, who was: Trajan had inherited the status from his father, one of those whom Vespasian had made patrician.[55]

Patrician status, or the lack of it, also helps to shed light on the mystery surrounding the accession of Hadrian in 117. On that occasion the adoptive principle pretty certainly had not been invoked, unless one is to believe the unconvincing tale told by Trajan's widow to the effect that Trajan had adopted Hadrian on his death-bed. Trajan's failure, right down to the time of his death, to indicate Hadrian as his successor calls for explanation. Hadrian was Trajan's nearest male relative, was of the right age, and furthermore had had a great deal of military and administrative experience, so that the nomination of him would have been in the natural order of things. Yet Trajan had not chosen him. Trajan, of course, must have known of, and disapproved of, Hadrian's opposition to territorial expansion. That was enough to give Trajan pause; and, so long as he himself did not make Hadrian patrician, he could always aver that Hadrian because of his non-patrician status was not of the stuff of which emperors ought to be made. Incidentally, Hadrian's non-patrician status is not in any doubt: he had actually held the office of plebeian tribune and in his vigintivirate days had not been one of the mint-masters.[56] Perhaps Trajan was hoping that some alternative to Hadrian would ultimately be forthcoming. If that was his hope, it was frustrated by his own comparatively early death in 117; whereupon Hadrian inevitably became emperor. It was hardly an uneventful succession. Hadrian, of course, could claim that his 'adoption' by Trajan automatically made him a patrician.[57] But he needed more reassurance than that. Accordingly four of the most illustrious ex-consuls in the Roman Empire were executed. Perhaps it had been from them that Trajan had been hoping to find his alternative to Hadrian. At the very least it seems likely that the four men had been opposed to the elevation of one whom they knew to be planning the surrender of the conquests that they themselves had helped Trajan to win. The charge against them was the inevitable one of 'conspiracy,' although how four men widely spearated from one another could have hatched a conspiracy in such short order it is not easy to see.[58]

Hadrian was hardly likely to forget how his own lack of lofty lineage had prejudiced his chances for the succession, and he bore it very much in mind later when his own turn came to name a successor. Undoubtedly patrician birth was not then for him the only consideration: he was determined to find a successor who could be trusted to continue his own antiexpansionist programme. Hadrian's natual choice could have been expected to be Pedanius Fuscus, his only adult male relative and, as it happened, a patrician to boot. But Hadrian evidently suspected that young man of harbouring the same imperialist instincts as his aged grandfather Julius Servianus. Julius Servianus had been one of Trajan's principal collaborators in territorial expansion and years before had quarrelled violently with Hadrian, who was his brother-in-law, presumably on that very issue.[59] To clear the way for securely anti-imperialist successors Hadrian hounded Pedanius Fuscus and Julius Servianus to their deaths in 136.[60] He then proceeded to adopt a patrician notorious for his good looks and luxurious habits, who could not by even the wildest stretch of the imagination be regarded as a military man.[61] L. Ceionius Commodus, before his adoption under the name of L. Aelius Caesar, seems never to have seen a legion in his life. The same can also be said of Antoninus Pius, whom Hadrian chose next, after Ceionius Commodus' sudden death. Neither adoption was popular at the time, and it is to be noted that Hadrian felt it safe to ignore non-patricians whose services to the Empire had been far greater; Catilius Severus, for instance, who had been Antoninus' colleague in the consulship in 120. Widely different though the predilections of Hadrian made their fortunes, Julius Servianus, Pedanius Fuscus, Ceionius Commodus, and Antoninus Pius were all alike in one respect: they were all patricians. Hadrian had learned the lesson well. His search was for a pacifist, but it had to be a patrician pacifist.

The dispositions he made when he selected Antoninus Pius emphasize this even more strongly. Antoninus himself was a patrician: modern scholars are agreed on that, and they suggest that his family may have acquired the status under the Flavians.[62] But, at the time of his adoption by Hadrian, Antoninus appears to have had no surviving son of his own.[63] Hadrian therefore obliged him to remedy the deficiency by adopting not just one, but two youths. One of the two was Antoninus' nephew by marriage who is known to history as Marcus Aurelius, and the other was Ceionius Commodus' son, who is known to history as Lucius Verus. The parallel with AD 4, when Augustus adopted Tiberius and obliged Tiberius in his turn to adopt his own nephew Germanicus and his own stepson Agrippa Postumus, has been frequently remarked and is in truth blatant and palpable enough. Evidently Hadrian was intent upon founding a dynasty and wanted to make sure that it would adhere to his non-expansionist policies. But what induced him to select precisely these two youths as the eventual successors Of Antoninus? The dutiful character of the sixteen-year-old Marcus Aurelius is sufficient explanation in his case: Marcus Aurelius could safely be trusted to do his best to carry out Hadrian's wishes. But what could

Hadrian have known about the outlook of the seven-year-old Lucius Verus, who incidentally seems to have been the greater favourite of the two with him?[64] Perhaps Hadrian was trusting Antoninus and Marcus between them to train Lucius Verus along the right lines. Be that as it may, it is to be noted that Marcus Aurelius and Lucius Verus were both patricians, and this must have been a decisive factor in their selection.

Hadrian was succeeded, in due course and in turn, by Antoninus Pius, Marcus Aurelius, Lucius Verus, and Marcus Aurelius' son Commodus, patricians all; and the question of the succession did not arise again until Commodus was assassinated on the last day of the year 192. His death, like that of Nero about a century and a quarter earlier, not only brought a dynasty to an end together with the official abolition of the memory of its last unworthy member, but also ushered in a year of murderous rivalries and military chaos.

As usual, *inter arma silent leges*: and amid the violence of 193 aristocratic birth received but scant consideration. It was military might that decided, and none of the contenders for the purple was patrician. Helvius Pertinax and Didius Julianus were the first to make their pretensions good, and they did so with the backing of the Praetorian Guard. But in this kind of horseplay the pampered praetorians were no match for the legions, and their nominees got very short shrift: the legions had other ideas. The three biggest legionary armies in the Roman Empire at that time had each its own pretender. The army of Pannonia proclaimed Septimius Severus, that of Syria Pescennius Niger, and that of Britain Clodius Albinus.

The Senate could do little more than look on helplessly,[65] but the little that it did is revealing. As none of the pretenders was patrician,[66] it would not recognize any one of them unless and until he came to

Rome and compelled it to do so by *force majeure*; and Pescennius Niger and Clodius Albinus never got to Rome.

From this bloody rivalry, as we all know, it was Septimius Severus who emerged as the ultimate victor, after the elimination of Niger, followed a few years later by a particularly bloody encounter with the troops of Albinus near Lugdunum in Gaul. Septimius was an African with little, if any, Italian blood in his veins,[67] and it is significant that, to legitimize his seizure of power, he pretended to be a Roman patrician. As soon as he could, he put forward the cool claim that Marcus Aurelius had adopted him some fifteen years earlier, and this, of course, made him, Septimius, the son of a *divus* and the brother of a *damnatus*, both of them patricians; and Septimius pushed this fraudulent claim to preposterous lengths. He revoked the official ban on the memory of his 'brother,' the unspeakable Commodus, and had him officially deified instead; and he insisted that the name of his own son and intended successor, the monster known to history as Caracalla, should be Antoninus, after his adoptive 'grandfather,' Antoninus Pius. In fact Antoninus was the name by which Caracalla was henceforth officially known, right down to the day of his death, and even beyond.[68]

With the dynasty of the Severi the Roman Empire was well embarked upon the third century of its existence and was fast approaching the perilous time of troubles that was to transform Augustus' reorganization of the Roman state. After the assassination of Severus Alexander in 235, seizure of power by military adventurers became the order of the day. None of these soldier upstarts lasted long and few of them could boast of distinguished birth. Their one qualification was their sword; and it made very little difference if they were not patricians, or even senators. They asserted their claim by armed might, oblivious to all other considerations.

The violence of these so-called Barrack Emperors proved fatal to the hereditary patriciate of Rome that Augustus had snatched from the brink of extinction over two and a half centuries earlier: the last emperor positively known to have created new patricians was precisely Severus Alexander.[69] Yet even in those terrible days of military anarchy when the proud old institution was rapidly nearing its end, the desirability of patrician birth for a Roman emperor was not entirely forgotten. In 238 when the Senate found itself, once again and quite unexpectedly, faced with the necessity of selecting an emperor, it did not look further than the ranks of the patricians; and for good measure it named not one, but two of them, Balbinus and Pupienus, the former from a family that Hadrian had elevated and the latter from one that owed its distinction to Septimius Severus.[70]

Thus, during the greatest days of the Roman Empire, patrician rank was clearly a matter of some consequence. It helped to create emperors, and it encouraged men to become pretenders; and the uprising of patricians like Scribonianus and Saturninus, it will be remembered, led Claudius and Domitian into courses of action that affected the whole of subsequent history. Augustus had revived something that counted for much in Roman eyes.

Even the chaos of the half century between 235 and 285, fatal though it was to the hereditary patriciate, did not erase its memory. When the emperor Constantine, early in the fourth century, wished to honour those of his supporters whom he chiefly esteemed, the title that he chose for them was Patrician. This did not mean that, like Augustus before him, he was seeking to bring a dying institution back to life. He was conferring a personal distinction upon his nominees: he was not making them members of a continuing, hereditary aristocracy.[71] His Patricians look much more like the life-peers of the United

Kingdom of today than like the old hereditary peerage of England. But their title at least was taken directly from the aristocractic caste of Rome's earliest history; and every student of the fourth and fifth centuries AD will be familiar with the splendid services which non-hereditary Patricians, many of them very un-Roman in their origin, men like the great Aetius, for instance, rendered to the Roman Empire, postponing its disintegration and keeping alive its continuing magnetism.

If today one visits the Palatine Hill in Rome and enters the little museum that is housed there in what was once the Convent of the Visitation, a broken marble basin of the fifth century after Christ is one of the first objects to catch the eye. It was found on the Palatine and it is inscribed with the name of the man to whom it belonged: a certain Flavius Arbazagius, described on it as *comes et patricius*.[72] The flamboyant name proves that he was no Roman of the ancient stock: it points rather to an origin from the east, from Armenia perhaps.[73] Yet he had made his mark to such good purpose in the Roman state that he had been named one of its Patricians. A patrician of the late Roman Empire, and a Patrician from the eastern provinces at that, at the very spot where Rome had had its earliest small beginnings over twelve centuries earlier, is a phenomenon well able to arouse romantic and nostalgic sentiments. But the *comes et patricius* Flavius Arbazagius does more than catch the passing fancy. He graphically emphasizes the two aspects of the Roman Empire that more than all others impress the modern student: its cosmopolitanism and its durability. And if, in our contemplation of the Roman patriciate, we are able thus to be fascinated by a sense of continuity and tradition, this is duc to the political agility of the statesman who ensured the strong and wide survival of this most Roman of institutions: Augustus the patrician.

NOTES

1. Tac. *Ann.* 11.25; Suet. *Jul. Caes.* 41; Dio 43.47.8.
2. Dio 49.43.6: possibly Dio has made an error.
3. Dio 52.42.5.
4. Suet. *Aug.* 50.
5. For Augustus' new patricians see H. C. Heiter, *De Patriciis Gentibus Quae Imperii Romani Saeculis I, II, III Fuerint* (Diss. Berlin, 1909), pp. 41-55.
6. Vell. 2.74.4; Sen. *De Clem.*, 1.11; Suet. *Aug.* 15; App. *Bell. Civ.* 5.48, 49; Dio 48.14.4.
7. For Augustus' Veliternan origin see Suet. *Aug* 1, 94; Dio 45.1.1.
8. Vell. 2.60.1.
9. See Dio 45.6.2; 53.17.10.
10. Tac. *Ann.* 3.56.
11. *Res. Gest.* 6.24; Ovid, *Fasti* 2.127f.; Dio 55.10.10, cf. 56.9.3.
12. Dio 52.42.5.
13. Through Iulus, son of Aeneas and consequently grandson of Venus.
14. Suet. *Galba* 2.
15. Plebeians had been eligible for the consulship ever since 367 BC, but it was only since 342 that both of the consuls might be plebeian: Livy 6.35.5; 7.42.2.
16. See, for instance, R. Syme, *The Roman Revolution* (Oxford, 1939), *passim* and E. Badian, *Foreign Clientelae* (Oxford, 1958), *passim*.
17. *Fasti Consulares* ad an. 172: *ambo primi de plebe*.
18. E. T. Salmon in *Revue des études latines* 47 bis, 1969, pp. 321-4.
19. For the numbers of the patricians at different periods see A. Momigliano in *Oxford Classical Dictionary*[2] s.v. Patricians, p. 790.
20. See below, notes 28, 29, 30.
21. Syme, *Tacitus* (Oxford, 1958), pp. 574, 577, 579.
22. For Romulus as the original creator of the patricians see Plut. *Rom.* 13; *Quaest. Roman.* 58: Festus p. 454L. For Augustus as the new Romulus see Suet. *Aug.* 7, 95; Dio 46.46.3; 47.19.3; 53.16.5.
23. A. D. Nock in *CAH* 10, p. 479.
24. Ovid, *Tristia* 4.10.6.
25. Dio 46.45.
26. *Res Gest.* 1.7.

27. Dio 43.23.6; 48.20.2.
28. Dio 43.47.3.
29. Heiter pp. 40 f.
30. Dio 46.22.3.
31. For the favouritism enjoyed by patricians in office-holding see Heiter p. 6.
32. On the obscurity of Agrippa's origin see Vell. 2.96.
33. See note 5 above.
34. *ILS* 212 and Tac. *Ann.* 11.24.
35. Heiter pp. 55-8.
36. W. Eck, *Senatoren von Vespasian bis Hadrian* (Munich, 1970), pp. 108 f.
37. The expression *divide et impera* is, however, a Renaissance rather than a Roman one.
38. *PIR*^{2} 2, p. 71, no. 295.
39. Heiter p. 44.
40. Syme, *The Roman Revolution*, p. 498.
41. Dio 53.17.10; nor was it unknown to Dio's contemporary, Herodian (see 8.8.1).
42. Agrippa was ashamed of his humble origin: Sen. *Controv.* 2.4.13.
43. Tac. *Hist.* 2.48.
44. Heiter p. 57.
45. He came from the Sabine country: Suet. *Vesp.* 1.
46. Syme, *Tacitus*, p. 598.
47. Perhaps from Spain: Syme, *Tacitus*, p. 791.
48. Tac. *Hist.* 3.68.
49. See Mommsen, *Römisches Staatsrecht* 2.789.
50. Heiter p. 53.
51. On the mediocrity of Nerva's career before he became emperor see Syme, *Tacitus*, pp. 1 f.
52. Dio 68.4.
53. R. M. Geer in *TAPA* 67 (1936), pp. 47-54.
54. This may be the implication of Aur. Vict. *Epit.* 13.7 and even of Pliny, *Paneg.* 7.3.
55. Eck p. 109.
56. S.H.A. *Had.* 2, 3.
57. The 'adoption' is described in S.H.A. *Had.* 4.
58. Palma was at Tarracina, Celsus at Baiae, Nigrinus at Faventia, and Lusius on his way home from Mauretania: S.H.A. *Had.* 7.
59. On the relations between Hadrian and Servianus see Syme,

Tacitus, p. 600.

60. S.H.A. *Had.* 15, 23.

61. S.H.A. *Had.* 23; *Ael.* 5.

62. *PIR*² 1, p. 310, no. 1513; W. Hüttl, *Antoninus Pius* (Prague, 1936), p. 3; Syme, *Tacitus*, p. 595, n. 3; Eck, pp. 108 f.

63. But doubts about his lack of a son have been raised: Hüttl, p. 3.

64. On Hadrian's predilection for the boy Lucius Verus see S.H.A. *Ael* 7.2..

65. It is, of course, true that the Senate approved of Pertinax; but the fact remains that it was the Praetorians who took the initiative in making him emperor.

66. It is significant, however, that those of them that got the chance to do so (Pertinax, Didius Julianus, Septimius Severus) promptly had themselves made patrician.

67. On the possibility that Septimius Severus had some Italians among his forebears see A. R. Birley, *Septimius Severus, The African Emperor* (London, 1971), pp. 26-43.

68. In fact Antoninus became a name for Roman emperors long to conjure with: see Syme, *Emperors and Biography* (Oxford, 1971), pp. 78-88.

69. Heiter p. 4.

70. On the patrician status of both Pupienus and Balbinus see Syme, *Emperors and Biography*, pp. 172 f.

71. On the patriciate under Constantine see B. Kübler in *RE* 18 (1949), s.v. 'patres, patricii,' cols. 2231 f.; R. MacMullen, *Constantine* (New York, 1969), pp. 155, 193; A. Momigliano, *loc. cit.* (note 19); J. H. Smith, *Constantine the Great* (London, 1971), p. 273.

72. *CIL* 6.31978.

73. See O. Seeck in *RE* 2 (1895), s.v. 'Arbazacius,' col. 407.

Lucius Sulla: The Deadly Reformer

ERNST BADIAN

It is by now an outstanding honour to be invited to give a lecture in this series, which has established itself as among the leaders in its field – a worthy memorial to Professor Todd, who, quite apart from his own meritorious work on the novel, laid the foundations of the international standing that this University has acquired in the study of both Latin and Ancient History. Since Professor R. E. Smith, then Professor of Latin here, inaugurated the series with one of his best papers, there have been five lecturers. They comprise an Oxford Professor, two Cambridge Professors, a Provost of King's, three Knights and a CBE. And here am I, a resident alien in the United States and a Professor at a university only founded as such in 1948, standing in the same place. If I cannot equal the performance of my predecessors (and let me, without disparaging the others, pay a special tribute to the outstanding one of Professor Sir Ronald Syme), I must at least attempt to justify the honour you have paid me by choosing a subject that is surely second to none in the field of Roman history in both importance and interest.

It should now be a truism that the historian must not claim to give the explanation of a complex historical phenomenon. Such questions as, 'What were the causes of the Great War?' (or, 'of the fall of the Roman Republic?') – expecting, by implication, a list of neatly defined items – such questions are by now relegated to the privacy of the tutorial or the examination room, where the historian is shielded from the critical eye of his professional colleagues. But it is the historian's legitimate task to single out some of the strands in the complex weave and to trace their importance in the pattern; and it is in this humbler frame of mind that he will most usefully perform his proper task of letting the present and the past illuminate each other.

The story of Lucius Sulla arouses interest on many counts. The ruthless adventurer and sinister tyrant, transformed by success into a revered statesman, with (perhaps) uneasy doubts coming to gnaw at the faithful after his death – that figure is familiar in our age, so much so that we need hardly mention names; even though, as far as we can tell, the pattern repeats itself without becoming familiar to contemporaries.[1] Interest is added by the nature of our sources, which have bedevilled the study of Sulla more than that of most Roman leaders of the Republic. Sulla wrote an autobiography, which he finished towards the end of his life; and this far from unbiased document was one of the main sources of information of his later biographer Plutarch, and has left noticeable traces in Appian and (as far as we can tell) in Livy. The effect was reinforced by the interested panegyric of an eminent contemporary, long renowned as the most accomplished Roman historian up to his time, L. Cornelius Sisenna, who joined Sulla's victorious cause at a late stage and made up for tardiness by enthusiasm. For the period from the Social War down to Sulla's victory, his account was never superseded except (perhaps) by Livy, who is demonstrably based on him to a considerable extent.[2] Posterity, while in principle sometimes prepared to concede the bias (and sometimes eager to defend it), has in practice been happy to accept what was offered, meeting revaluation with shocked resistance. But for better or for worse, the historian cannot abdicate his responsibility.

Lucius Cornelius Sulla, born (probably) 138 BC,[3] was of ancient patrician lineage – of that immemorial aristocracy which went back to the origins of the city and beyond – and he was proud of it. In his autobiography, he seems to have devoted about two books to the story of his ancestors.[4] One ancestor, in the direct line, was P. Cornelius Rufinus, twice consul and dictator in the time of the Samnite and Pyrrhic Wars, who was expelled from the Senate by his enemy C. Fabricius – it was said, for owning more than ten pounds of silver plate.[5] The family tradition obviously included luxury! Rufinus' expulsion meant political eclipse for his immediate descendants, though social eminence was retained: his son, it seems, was *flamen Dialis* (a post that, while conferring high rank, almost debarred its holder from political activity),[6] and that priest's son began the slow climb back to power by being praetor; of his sons, two reached the same level. It was the elder of these two men – a great-grandson of Rufinus – who was the dictator's grandfather: this P. Sulla was praetor in 186. The family was settled in praetorian status for generations, but (it seemed) unable to advance any higher, like so many families, old and new, at all periods of the Republic.[7] Of L. Sulla's father we know nothing. He himself is said to have spent his youth in dire poverty; yet his father married (after L. Sulla's mother) a wealthy wife, who later left her stepson a fortune; and the young man, of course, had a literary and Greek education such as befitted one of his class.[8] His poverty and his father's obscurity may be exaggerated: one would think that a son, grandson and great-grandson of praetors, who in (at earliest) his second marriage landed an heiress, must have got somewhere in life and must have had more than a name to offer her family. He probably held some public office – even a praetorship need not surprise us, in the period for which we lack Livy's evidence. As for his son's biographers, the *peripeteia* of the self-made man, especially if (paradoxically) he is of high birth, has always been the stock-in-trade of romantic biography; nor was it unknown even to autobiography. While Sulla was a boy, another patrician, of more obviously decayed family, had been making his way to the top with single-minded ambition, to become Senior Senator and, for twenty-five years, politically perhaps the most powerful man of his generation. M. Aemilius Scaurus did not let people forget his success. At the beginning of his own autobiography (probably written in the nineties) he stressed the fact that his father had left him practically nothing: six slaves and 35,000 sesterces.[9] Only a few years later, Sulla completed an autobiography. The emphasis on his poor beginnings need not surprise us. It may be presumed – as fitting in with his later character – that he also took pride in his dissolute life. Plutarch gives us the name or *nom de guerre* of a wealthy prostitute whose will provided Sulla with another fortune. (She was called Nicopolis.) We have not far to look for the origin of that story. More interesting would be some indication of the more respectable women in his life: his mother and particularly the wealthy stepmother. However, Plutarch, demonstrably using Sulla's autobiography, does not give us this information. This is unfortunate: it might well explain some puzzling facts.[10]

As Sallust tells us, and Plutarch confirms, Sulla did no military service in his youth,[11] which meant he had no political ambitions; and he seems to have held no junior office: Plutarch knows almost nothing about him before his quaestorship. Then suddenly, in 108, we find Sulla taken from the midst of his disreputable companions and walking straight into a quaestorship.[12] Of course, it may have been at this time that he acquired his fortune by double inheritance; but there might be more to it. For 108 was the year when a new man won a surprising consulship after a demagogic canvass, to succeed in due course to the command in Numidia; and it was precisely to C. Marius that Sulla was assigned as a quaestor.[13] Marius is said to have been shocked to find himself saddled with a quaestor who had left the tavern and the brothel only to attend to his election. He was the man who had attacked the decadence of the nobility, and, whatever his faults, he took soldiering seriously. No wonder he now cursed his luck.

But stay: how did he treat this young man totally without military experience[14] whom the lot had foisted upon him? The answer may surprise. That shrewd soldier, concerned to make a success of the war if he was to have a political future, left the inexperienced young libertine to levy cavalry in Italy and bring them over to Africa; there, he led them in the battle of Cirta, guarded Marius' camp, and was indeed shown every sign of respect and confidence, until he was finally sent to take charge of the nerve-racking negotiations that led to the surrender of Jugurtha by Bocchus. Surely, right from the start, responsible tasks for a man whom one had reason to distrust. It leads us to wonder about the coincidence which, in the very year that saw C. Marius' flamboyant rise to the consulship, promoted this young patrician, with hitherto no thought of a political or military career, to a quaestorship and the chance to show his talents. The consul elect, triumphantly swept into power, might well have a say in the election of the quaestor who was to attend him in a major war; and although quaestorian *prouinciae* were normally settled by lot, we know that it was perfectly proper for a commander to pick his quaestor.[15] Perhaps this conjecture – for it can be no more – begins to make sense of the story. The sudden rise of the loose-living young patrician may not by mere accident parallel that of the cunning *nouus homo*. Marius – a snob like all new men – had a soft spot for patricians; it was not many years since he had married a young lady of impeccable patrician birth, but with no consul among her direct ancestors. And he was on the look-out for talent, trying to build up a personal following for the future.[16]

The confidence shown strongly suggests previous acquaintance, indeed political clientship. Again, it might help to know whom Sulla's father married. It may once more not be by accident that we lack this information: did Sulla choose not to mention his mother's or stepmother's name when he wrote about his youth? Certainly, if there were a connection with Marius, it could not be mentioned when the work was prepared for publication, a generation later.[17]

In any case, the connection now continues, visibly played down by Sulla in his autobiography, as indeed we should expect. Marius, we are told, disliked the way in which Sulla claimed credit for the victory over Jugurtha by having a signet-ring engraved with the scene of the surrender.[18] Yet when Marius was sent out, as consul for a second time, to fight the Germans, Sulla again served under him as legate.[19] In the following year (103), he continued to serve as a military tribune, an office unparalleled in that generation, at this late stage of a man's life and career. Whatever the reason for this – a special task in a difficult legion, or merely another office to aid Sulla in his later career? – it shows a remarkably close connection between the two men. Naturally, Plutarch is puzzled at the contradiction, having just told us the story of the boastful ring. He suggests a solution: Marius' continued confidence was a sign of contempt, showing that he thought Sulla not worthy of his jealousy. The solution is worthy of his source and, for all we know, may go back to it. Indeed, the difficult source situation that we have noted here shows its advantage for the alert historian: it helps to know what was thought worth disguising, where it could not be suppressed.

Distortion now continues and obfuscation becomes more patent. Marius, annoyed at Sulla's brilliant successes (would he, in a war as vital to his own future as to his country's, have wanted his officer actually to fail?), now stopped giving him important assignments, and so Sulla left his service and joined the army of Q. Lutatius Catulus, the other consul of 102. For Catulus – a worthy man, but not a great soldier, as Sulla (explicity quoted in this context) later described him – he performed outstanding services, saving him from disaster; and at this Marius grew thoroughly envious. From such small causes, Plutarch adds, do bloody civil wars take their origin.

Perhaps. But some facts are worth recalling. Q. Catulus was Marius' special protégé, owing everything to him: after three failures, he had reached the consulship when Marius' prestige stood at its highest, and he was closely related to the Caesares, Marius' relatives by marriage. As consul, he was allowed by Marius to take over part of the German War (which no other colleague of Marius had been or was to be), and even though his success in this was at the best dubious, Marius, entitled to two clear triumphs, magnanimously shared a single one with Catulus.[20] Even if Sulla had been entitled to leave his commander without asking for permission,[21] it is clear that Catulus could not have accepted him in such a case – and had he done so, Marius was not one who would lightly forgive. In fact, the patrician libertine and the noble perennial loser make a good pair: both raised to eminence by the great *nouus homo*, whose methods in providing for his political future are characteristic. Having landed himself with a colleague politically useful, but militarily inept, Marius had to make sure that disaster did not follow. It is not surprising that he did so by ceding to him the man who had throughout his military career been Marius' most trusted and (presumably) most loyal subordinate. By his own account, Sulla at least prevented disaster and made the gesture of the joint triumph possible. This story, again, could not be told twenty years later; it is not too difficult to retrieve.

Nor is this as yet the end of the story. It can be shown, I think, that Sulla's failure to gain a praetorship in 99 and his success in 98 are not due merely to a difference in the size of the bribes, as Plutarch (i.e. Sulla) tries to make us believe: home from the successful wars, Sulla was not short of money on the first occasion. Scrutiny of the political background appears to show Sulla still involved in Marius' fortunes, with its ups and downs.[22] When and how did opposition to Marius start? The massive distortion of the sources makes it impossible to tell. But perhaps we have a clue. After a most successful promagistracy in 96-5, when he restored a king to his throne and was the first Roman to receive a Parthian embassy,[23] he was prosecuted for extortion on his return. Now, his prosecutor, C. Marcius Censorinus, was later a prominent partisan of Marius and Cinna in the first civil war. This is not conclusive for 95; but it might be a pointer that Sulla was already on the other side. Moreover, Censorinus soon abandoned the prosecution – always an extraordinary action to take. Cicero calls him 'lazy and hating legal business';[24] if this were the whole answer, why had he started on the case? No, the whole affair must fit into the battle of prosecutions in the middle nineties, which (as I once tried to show) very largely involved the *dignitas* of Marius, and which ended in a stalemate.[25] And if there is anything at all in Plutarch's remark about Marius' jealousy over Sulla's success under Catulus (but we cannot be sure of this), it might follow that it was the gradually developing hostility between Marius and Catulus (arising out of rivalry over the claim to have defeated the Germans) that forced Sulla to take sides – and made him take the side that promised to be the winning one.[26] But whatever the background, Sulla's luck, of which he was later so proud, now left him: he did not stand for the consulship, and this, in view of his single-minded ambition hitherto,[27] must mean that he had no chance. We can only note the fact. I doubt if we have enough information on the politics of the nineties to attempt an interpretation.

We know, however, that it was in 92 that the political situation was brought to the boil by the conviction of P. Rutilius Rufus. This distinguished ex-consul, lawyer and philosopher, who had merely helped the proconsul Q. Mucius Scaevola to keep the exploitation of Asia by Roman financiers under control, was driven into exile after an outrageous political trial, which disgraced the class of wealthy non-senators who were in charge of the criminal juries and showed that the whole immemoiral practice of senatorial control of the state was in jeopardy.[28] Even the most innocent senator, and even the most dignified, now had to fear prosecution; and the cases were not slow in starting.[29] The result was the tribunate of M. Livius Drusus, backed by some of the most eminent nobles (chief of them M. Aemilius Scaurus, the Senior Senator), who hoped to solve all the major problems of the state in a grand scheme of reforms.[30]

The results of that eventful year 91 BC are beyond our immediate concerns. It was a year of turmoil, with Senate and People divided within themselves, and violence always in the air. This was the time when Sulla thought his hour had come: the leading men in the state were getting old, and there might be a chance for a new generation. He decided to stake his claim to eminence, and to leadership against Marius – a cause that would be popular in the best circles, since Marius, out of personal bitterness and disappointment, had supported the prosecution of P. Rutilius Rufus:[31] it was he, linked with the leaders of the wealthy nonsenatorial circles (the 'equites,' as they were later called) throughout his life, who could be blamed for the danger to the state and for the violence. And so it was now, apparently late in 91,[32] that Bocchus dedicated on the Capitol a group of statues showing Sulla's favourite scene: the surrender of Jugurtha to him. Not unpredictably, Marius was enraged: at this time and in the circumstances of that year, the act was a slap in the face for him. He threatened to remove the offending objects – a contingency that Sulla probably faced with equanimity, since it would have been a hideous act of sacrilege that could not have failed to bring Sulla massive support. The incident is fully reported in Plutarch, but it has again failed to puzzle the incurious: recent works appear to remain silent. Yet as we survey Bocchus' innocent gesture, we must recall that a foreigner did not simply walk into Rome's most sacred temple and leave some statues there. Before an offering could be dedicated, the Senate's permission had to be obtained.[33] Clearly, the King had obtained it.[34] This, however, restores the incident to its true importance: the slap in the face for Marius had been a formal one, fully intended by the senators who had voted for the dedication. It shows that Sulla had chosen his time and his issue wisely. It is safe to say that it marks the entry of Sulla as a serious consular candidate and as a claimant to factional leadership. He might well have been consul in 90 or at the worst 89, with luck and skill.

But for the moment his ambitions were overwhelmed by national disaster. Drusus' death was followed by the Social War, and national unity took precedence. Both Marius and Sulla distinguished themselves in the War.[35] But Marius, when he failed to achieve his aim of becoming the sole saviour of the Republic, retired in disgust. Sulla fought on, welding his army into a loyal personal following, by success and indulgence.[36] When the war was over, he had his reward: M. Scaurus was dead by now, and his widow (a Metella, of one of the most powerful families in Roman politics) married Sulla. This was offical recognition. Even before the marriage (though hardly before it was planned), Sulla had been elected consul for 88.[37] His colleague was Q. Pompeius Rufus, a man long connected with the circle of M. Livius Drusus, into which Sulla had now been adopted. Pompeius' son was married to Sulla's daughter. With startling clarity, the manipulation of Roman politics at crucial times stands revealed. With the Social War over, normal politics could resume its course. As in the case of the Hannibalic War, a century earlier, victory appeared to have been annexed by the Establishment, which proceeded to claim the political profits. Sulla had chosen the right side. But the consulship was a means to an end: war against Mithridates had broken out in the East, a war that had excited the ambition of several men, for there were cheap triumphs to be won in the East, and massive booty. Marius and one of his relatives by marriage, C. Caesar Strabo, had been quarrelling over this command, and towards the end of 89 the city had seen riots and street-fighting, in which a young tribune (also a friend of M. Livius Drusus and a powerful public speaker), P. Sulpicius Rufus, had taken a prominent part.[38] Now it was all over. The Establishment had intervened, and Sulla was its candidate – justifiably enough, both from the political point of view (in view of his activities just before the

Social War) and from the military (in view of his successes in the war itself). The consuls drew lots, and Fortune, ever on his side, awarded the eastern war to Sulla – to no one's surprise, one may think. He had won the game.

And then it all dissolved before his eyes. Rome after the Social War and a generation of *popularis* tradition was not going to return to aristocratic control as easily as had appeared. Having won, the faction shut its eyes to the dictates of equity and of prudence. When the tribune. P. Sulpicius proceeded to put a Drusan programme into effect by assuring the newly-enfranchised Italians of an equal distribution among the voting-tribes, his friend. Q. Pompeius, now consul, would have none of it: the state appeared to have happily settled down to oligarchic guidance, and reform could only endanger it. The Drusan programme, for those who had supported it as a mere means to an oligarchic end, was now out of date. Sulpicius, however, was a younger man, and (like M. Drusus himself) probably based his politics on moral conviction inextricably mixed with aristocratic pride. Deeply wounded in both by his friend's desertion, he made common cause with another embittered man and, as we are explicitly told, violently reversed his political attitude. In return for the support that Marius could still command, among the equites (both financiers and country squires) who were his own class and the veterans who had fought under him, Sulpicius promised the old man the eastern command. After all, Marius himself had set the precedent, in his first consulship, when the African command, given by the Senate to Metellus Numidicus, had been transferred to him by vote of the people.[39]

Sulla, who had earlier left the city in order to prepare for his departure overseas, returned to oppose the tribune. Fighting and rioting followed, in which Pompeius' son was killed, and finally the consuls left the city and Sulpicius passed his various laws, including the one transferring the command to Marius. Again, the sources pose a question: did Sulla, when his life was in danger during the riots, take refuge in Marius' house and come to terms with Marius, withdrawing opposition to the laws in return for a safe conduct and a guarantee of confirmation in office? Did he owe his life to this bargain and then repudiate it? Sulla, inevitably, later denied it. Fortunately, in this case he aroused Plutarch's curiosity by protesting too much. He claimed he had merely been driven towards Marius' house by an armed mob, and had then made his way back to the forum and renounced his opposition to the laws. In the *Marius*, Plutarch merely cites the two versions, non-committally. By the time he came to write the *Sulla*, he had found out another crucial point: after the consuls had left, Sulpicius, while passing a law deposing Q. Pompeius, took no such action against Sulla. There is no doubt that the bargain was struck.[40]

Grave portents were later remembered. Plutarch lists them. A mouse gnawed gold in a temple and, on being caught, gave birth in the trap and devoured three of her young; and the call of a trumpet was heard coming out of the sky. Tuscan seers calculated that a *saeculum* – even a Great Year of the Heavens – was drawing to an end. In the circumstances, Marius and Sulpicius were unwise to let Sulla escape on the strength of his word. For Sulla went straight to his army in Campania – the army he had led in the Social War and moulded into a personal following – before the government's agents could reach it. What he had to tell his men made good sense to them: Marius had been given the command, and if allowed to take it over, would not dream of taking them (his enemy's army) to the rich spoils of the East. Others would reap the harvest. They responded as Sulla had expected. The officers who came to take them over were stoned, and the army marched on

Rome.

It was, in a way, the result of a reform that Marius himself had introduced. It was he who, in his first consulship, had abandoned the immemorial principle that only people possessing a minimum of property should serve in the legions, and had opened the army to *proletarii*.[41] The action had undoubtedly helped to save the state in a series of military crises that could not have been met with the old resentful and numerically inadequate recruits. But he had created what we nowadays call the 'client army,' and it was Sulla who first saw its implications. The new class of the dispossessed in arms, mercenaries in their own country, now inured by the Social War to the devastation of Italy, had nothing to hope for but booty, and no one from whom to expect it but their leader. These men had no stake in the *res publica*. The traditional insistence on at least a minimum property qualification for anyone entrusted with arms and taught to use them had not been mere prejudice.

But if Marius had created a revolutionary force, he was not aware of it. Rioting for political ends was by now almost traditional, accepted by both sides, ever since 133 BC, as a regrettable part of the *res publica*. But no citizen army had ever marched on Rome. Appeals to abandon the impious attempt were in vain, and Marius and Sulpicius, caught completely by surprise, made their escape, with their followers, while Sulla occupied the city. Some of his enemies (including Sulpicius) were caught and executed and Sulpicius' laws repealed: Sulla once more had his command.

Victory, however, had been bought at a price. Sulla, hitherto heir to the leadership of the most powerful faction, found that even the very faction that had supported him was far from unanimously behind him now. Where the men enthusiastically followed him against

Rome, the officers (all except for a quaestor, probably his wife's relative L. Lucullus) had abandoned him to a man.[42] The Senate as a whole was hostile, the People cowed and resentful. The use of a private army of *proletarii* to set up a *regnum* did not arouse the enthusiasm of the upper class, nor the support of a People accustomed to their share of political power and its concrete advantages. The consuls (for Pompeius had returned with Sulla) had to send the army back to restore a semblance of legality before they could muster enough support to legislate with any hope of permanence: for unless they gained at least acquiescence, any measures they passed would simply be reversed when Sulla's army left for the East. A permanent armed occupation of Rome, even if it had been conceivable at this stage, was out of the question in the circumstances. However, with the army discreetly out of sight, various laws were passed. Unfortunately our tradition has confused them with Sulla's later reforms, and we cannot sort them out here; and since they did not long remain in force, it is not worth while, in this context. Such as we can discern them, they show Sulla still fumbling after a programme of reform.[43] Nor need we go into detail over what followed: Q. Pompeius' death at the hands of the first disciple of Sulla's, the father of Pompey the Great, who had the consul killed by his army which he unwisely came to take over in person; the election of a hostile consul for 87, L. Cinna; and the fact that Sulla had to permit both these blows, since the only alternative was to give up the eastern war and use his army in Italy. Now, the client army had proved loyal to its commander even against the state, provided he held out concrete hopes of booty. They might not follow him if he did not. If he failed to deliver as promised, they might leave him for a higher bidder, or simply go home. Sulla knew his men: he ignored Rome and Italy – the hostile consul, demonstrating the solid hostility of the well-to-do to the proletarian army and its leader,[44] and the hostile army so like his own – and left for the East. The future was to show that he was right. No sooner had he left Italy than Cinna tried to overturn his arrangements. Driven out of the city by the other consul, he went straight to Campania, to part (it seems) of that very army that Sulla had left there; for the Social War was by no means wholly concluded, and some troops had to stay behind. Without the slightest difficulty Cinna gained their allegiance, to follow him to Rome. Sulla, leaving them behind, had disappointed them; the next man would do as well.[45]

Sulla accurately gauged the forces that he had unleashed in the state. But he had another reason for leaving. In the East, Greece might be overrun by the enemy if he delayed – or so he might claim. The truth, perhaps, was worse. Again the sources are confused.[46] A legate of the governor of Macedonia had been fighting against the 'Eastern hordes' of Mithridates, and there is good reason to think that he had defeated them and driven them back to the sea. If this is the right version of the story, then Sulla had reason to hurry: if he waited, his men might be altogether cheated of their victory and he himself of his projected military base. He would have only rapid conviction to expect. That this was the situation seems to be confirmed by the fact that Sulla at once ordered the legate to withdraw and leave the war to him. And confident of victory where a lesser man with smaller forces had been successful, he crossed to Greece and duly won it.

In Italy, meanwhile, Cinna received the aid of Marius, whose name was still worth legions, and after bitter resistance captured Rome. The disintegration of the Republic had advanced another step. The war with the Italians had brought devastation to peninsular Italy, for the first time since Hannibal. Sulla had seized Rome with a

Roman army, for the first time in its history. Now, for the first time, Rome was attacked, defended, and captured after siege, all by citizen soldiers. There followed a massacre worse than Sulla's. The end of Rome seemed in sight.

However, at this point Marius died, within days of assuming his seventh consulship. Cinna was left to govern and set himself the task of trying to bring the state back to health, to restore order and confidence. For the leaders of political life, the choice was difficult: were they to stay and co-operate with the régime that had taken Rome by force and ruled it by terror? If not, what could they do? Join Sulla, who had set the precedent of doing just that? Several of the best-known men departed for various provinces, where they could keep out of the limelight. Even Q. Metellus Pius, head of the Metelli, the family that had adopted Sulla and helped him attain the consulship and the command, now chose this course as preferable to joining Sulla. No man of real consequence joined the demagogue who had led his mercenary army against Rome. In fact, all the ex-consuls (the senior statesmen who decided policy) and many other eminent men chose to stay and co-operate, in the hope of restoring peace and stability. Cinna now embarked, with fair success, on a programme of peace and reconciliation, which I have tried to follow elsewhere.[47] Before long it was clear that legitimate government was returning to Rome, and Sulla too was given a chance to co-operate, and to argue out his differences with the government after the foreign enemy had been defeated. For the moment he accepted: his forces in Greece and the government forces sent to Asia did not clash. But in fact he was soon faced with the same situation as in late 88. A vigorous offensive by those forces was winning Asia itself from Mithridates; soon the war would be won – by L. Sulla; and what then? He had his answer. Making peace with the man who had slaughtered 80,000 Italians in Asia, and recognizing him as an ally, he helped him clear Asia of the army of the Senate and People of Rome; and when his own troops grumbled at this, he again knew the answer, from long experience. He let them spend a winter quartered on the wealthy cities of Asia. There was never another murmur. Sulla knew his men.

And then Sulla's luck (that Fortune which he proclaimed and believed was always ultimately on his side)[48] reasserted itself, decisively. Cinna, preparing for a campaign in Illyria, to train an army that might (if called upon) be able to face Sulla's veterans,[49] was killed in a mutiny. It was one of those accidents that decide great issues, far more often than some historians like to admit. Compromise had failed and the government quickly disintegrated. At once various eminent nobles (including Q. Metellus) who had been in hiding in the provinces rose in arms and collected forces against the government. In Italy, a young man, Cn. Pompeius (later Pompey the Great), called on his father's veterans, who had not minded murdering a consul, and enrolled a legion against the government in the heart of the country. In Rome itself, more and more of the leading men drifted away.

Sulla never missed a chance. Leaving Asia, with the supplies that his ally Mithridates had given him, he made for Greece, and late in 83 he crossed over to Italy. By then, many of the eminent gentlemen who had hesitated for so long were with him. As he defeated the raw levies that (owing to Cinna's failure) were all that the government could put in the field against him, more flocked to him. The man who had been started on his career by Marius, and had joined his enemies; the rebel who had led a private army of proletarians against Rome and had occupied it; to the disgust and deep suspicion of all right-thinking citizens, the Roman commander who had sold the forces of the Senate and People to their greatest enemy and the murderer of thousands of Italians, in order to call that enemy in as his ally against his own country – this man, through success, suddenly became the hero and champion of the nobility, the defender of the state.[50] By late 82 he had conquered Rome. Now came the proscriptions – the reign of terror in which hundreds, perhaps thousands, were arbitrarily killed, and their property confiscated, without even a pretence of trial, at the mere whim of Sulla or (as often, it seems) of one of his subordinates, satisfying a private grudge or private greed. This time, unlike 88, Sulla did nothing to spare the feelings of senators or to soothe their consciences by a show of legality. It was clear that he did not think highly enough of his new friends to bother.

However, this could not last. Order had to be restored. During 81, with full 'dictatorial' authority that permitted him to do literally whatever he chose to, he reorganized the state by means of a programme of comprehensive reform. That programme is well known in outline, and too extensive to be discussed in detail on this occasion. But the fact as such is worth noting. The man who had seemed dedicated to war and personal ambition, ruthless and treacherous at home and in the field; who had spent his leisure in luxury, affecting the company of actors and prostitutes – that man now saw himself as the new Romulus,[51] refounding the city that he had brought to the verge of destruction. In 88 he had still been feeling his way, knowing that he had no assurance that his work would be lasting, and no time to make it coherent. This time he had a coherent plan, based, of course, on the ideas of the circle that had given him what political background he had – the circle of the Metelli, of M. Scaurus and M. Livius Drusus.[52] In outline it was simple enough: to intergrate the Italians into the state; to attach the People firmly to the guidance of the governing class, their traditional leaders; and to eliminate the irresponsible political power of the equites that had grown up since Gaius Gracchus.[53] But things had changed in the last ten years, and there were new problems to be solved, which M. Livius Drusus had not even been aware of. The new Republic had to be guarded against a host of dangers, and Sulla had thought of them all.

Here we might notice a striking aspect of the disintegration that marked the decline of the Roman Republic. Most of the time, it was not opposition to reform that destroyed the state (we have heard all about the load of guilt that attaches to those who opposed Tiberius Gracchus); it was reform itself. It was almost as though history had been out to confirm the forebodings of those traditional Optimates who saw anything new (*res nouae*) as a revolution and any change as a change for the worse. The process is perhaps a warning on the limitations of human foresight – limitations in no way due to the ancients' unfortunate ignorance of computer technology, but as real and obvious today as in antiquity. At each stage, even well-intentioned and genuine attempts to reform what seemed patent errors and abuses resulted in changes in the social and political balance that the reformer had not (perhaps could not have) foreseen. Tiberius, helpless against opposition, tried to find a way out by enhancing the power of a tribune supported by the People. That power remained, to plague the Republic henceforth. Tiberius, however, was killed, and his fate showed that deep-seated evils needed attention. One of them, in the eyes of his supporters, was the reliance on landed wealth as the sole qualification for political power.[54] Not only had it turned out to be the landed interest that prevented reform, but the cardinal principle of constitutional practice, that landed wealth could be regarded as alone sufficiently disinterested to be fit to rule, had been conspicuously proved false. Moreover, the power of the Senate in the *res publica* had been shown to be excessive.[55] C. Gracchus and his circle thought they had found the answer by introducing the whole class of wealthy citizens (including financial interests) into the political process: the court that sat in judgment on senators was put into their hands, thereby giving them a check and a countervailing power. These were the men who later came to fom the class called 'equites'. The result was (as the historian Varro put it[56]) 'to make the state two-headed' and to lead to serious discord. In 92, as we saw, the new class showed that it was a disturbing and not a regulating influence: power without responsibility, political leverage without political interests or indeed policies – this threatened to produce, in the literal sense, anarchy, to make the state ungovernable. Similarly the Italian problem. Introduced into Roman politics as a by-product of the Gracchan reform, as a tactical measure taken by the land commission to increase the amount of public land available for distribution;[57] made acute by the wars of the late second century, which led men to realize that equal sacrifice demanded equal recognition; it finally threatened to destroy the state. M. Drusus, using the methods made possible by Ti. Gracchus, tried to deal with both these new dangers that had developed out of the Gracchan reforms. The result was a major war with the allies and fierce hatreds within the body politic, demonstrated by the trials of 91-89.[58] Marius had tried to deal with the manpower shortage that threatened to make defence of the empire impossible and had extended the base of recruitment. The result, as we saw, was to provide a less scrupulous and less tradition-bound man with an instrument for capturing the Republic. The list could be extended. All the well-intentioned and (individually) necessary reforms of the generation since the Gracchi had fused to bring about the explosion that lasted from 91 to 80. Sulla had to start again.

One problem, that of the Italians, at least, was now out of the way. He had realized that the Italian upper class had to be used for stabilizing the Republic and not left as a threat outside it. As he had made clear some time after his landing,[59] the Italians retained their citizenship and at least in principle, were no longer confined to special tribes. (This, of course, in no way inhibited Sulla from arbitrarily punishing his enemies among them, as among citizens.[60]) The chief remaining problems, as he saw them, could be reduced to three: the demagogues who had set the People against the Senate; the existence of the equites, the new class that had power without responsibility; and – the problem that he naturally saw most clearly of all, and that marks the main change since the day of M. Drusus – the 'client army': if the state was to survive at all, he himself must have no imitators. Sulla, as we have seen, modelled his solution on the example of the circle of M. Drusus – perhaps along lines suggested by Drusus' teacher, the orator L. Crassus;[61] but with special regard to the new situation that he himself had created. All the problems could be seen as closely related: they could be subsumed under the heading of centrifugal tendencies, threatening disintegration. The answer was to give the state a single head again – and for a man like Sulla, indeed (we may say) for any Roman politician coming to that conclusion at that time, that head could only be the Senate. No other course was conceivable, and this is the basic thought behind the Sullan constitution. The Senate became supreme beyond challenge, in the legislative and judicial and, as far as possible, even in the executive and military sphere. The details all fit in with this guiding idea: the ban on tribunician initiative in the assembly; the laws binding provincial governors; the reconstitution and extension of the criminal courts; even the increases in the numbers of magistrates. For the ten provinces, two ex-consuls and eight ex-praetors were in principle to be available every year, so that change might normally be annual; and enough quaestors were created to serve them and fulfil all the other requirements.[62] Sulla's special attention was devoted to what had been the chief anarchic force of the nineties, the equites. The expanded courts were transferred to the Senate, so that the two-headedness created by C. Gracchus was now repaired. It was probably Sulla, as is generally recognized, who withdrew the privilege of sitting in fourteen specially designated rows of seats at spectacles from the equites.[63] However, the Senate, if only in order to be able to deal with the vastly increased activity, had to be raised to a membership of 600 (as M. Drusus had first seen). Since the establishment had earlier been about 300, and many had dropped out owing to the wars of the last decade, a large complement had to be found – and where could it come from except from (in the widest sense) the equites, the wealthy class outside the Senate?[64] Well over 300 must have been raised to the new Senate, all of them (of course) Sulla's men.

What happened to Sulla's opponents among that class is no secret. Large numbers were proscribed,[65] their property (the basis of their importance) confiscated and redistributed, and the men themselves either killed or, if they escaped, debarred (with their families) from public service. Thus, by the complementary processes of decimation and promotion, the class as a whole was deprived of its politically prominent elements, at the same time as it was deprived of power and conspicuous distinction as a class. No wonder nothing much is heard of the equites for a decade. Those left could be assumed to be dedicated to *otium* – the unimpeded pursuit of wealth and its enjoyment. The myth of Sulla's hatred for the equites has often been exposed: he did nothing to diminish their business opportunities and promoted a large number of their leaders to the Senate. But as a class, they were purged, with single-minded thoroughness, of any chance of political power.

The balanced constitution that Polybius had described with admiration in the middle of the second century, and that had perhaps been in the mind of C. Gracchus, had led to total disintegration, under the blows of reform and the consequences it progressively produced. Sulla was by no means an antiquarian or a romantic, as he is often depicted. His purpose was quite simply a political solution. He accepted recent constitutional developments, even extended them, and raised them to basic principles of his system: thus the criminal courts, and the practice of sending magistrates to their overseas provinces after rather than during their year of office.[66] In the face of this, it is absurd to speak (in any proper sense of the word) of 'reaction.' No received institution was too sacred for him: thus the tribunate was pruned back to a lower position than it had ever held in recorded history. On the other hand, Italians were freely admitted to the Senate, and the support of the upper classes of Italy was recognized as vital to the survival of the Republic. A balanced constitution could work only if there was *concordia*, and *concordia* could not be revived by force. It would have to grow, and Sulla probably hoped that his arrangements would give it time to do so. The Italian problem was solved: demagogues and ambitious generals were neutralized; the political differences between the two leading orders were significantly reduced by the adlection of so many eminent equites into the Senate: equestrian interests would not lack representation there. In fact, there was now little difference of background or interests between Senate and equites: Cicero later had good hopes for their *concordia*, and though moderns often look down on him as naive, he knew Roman politics better than most men.

Meanwhile, for the balance that had broken down and led to disintegration, Sulla substituted a new degree of legal centralization, with law reinforcing what custom had either been unable to ensure, or had never attempted to. This was far from reaction; we might describe it as a revolution, in a constitutional sense. And, clearly, Sulla meant it to work. For he at once began to dismantle the special powers he had taken. At the end of 81 (so far as we can see) he ceased to be dictator and in 80, as consul with an equal colleague (Q. Metellus Pius), he was no longer accompanied by twenty-four lictors, no longer supreme. When Cicero, in his speech defending Roscius of Ameria, appealed to him, in the course of that year, to assure the prestige of the aristocracy to which he had returned the state, the ambitious young man knew what Sulla would want to hear. By 79, Sulla was a private citizen, taking no interest in the elections for 78, except to announce his displeasure at the result.[67] Those to whom he had committed the state would have to learn to run it – supported, needless to say, by a ring of his veterans settled in colonies and on expropriated land, up and down Italy. The new *res publica* was assured of a fair start.

The personal 'enigma' of Sulla – an eternal subject of speculation and romance – is not for us to discuss here. The political enigma – that of his retirement – is an unnecessary puzzle, due, like many such, to modern myth building on ancient. Caesar – a very different man, in a very different situation – at a time when the Sullan Republic had shown that it was not viable could not understand Sulla's action;[68] later, it became a subject for debate in the schools, and as such it is still with us. In fact, he had no alternative. The time for military monarchy had not yet come – as even Caesar found out, a generation and a bloodbath later, when the Republic could in fact be seen to be dead. It took a great deal more slaughter to make it possible, and then by degrees, with caution and tact. Sulla had had his moment of *regnum*. What had long been a term of political abuse had briefly become reality. Perhaps the thought was not entirely absent, in Sulla's arbitrary cruelty and contempt for morality or public opinion, that reality should act as a deterrent. Sulla had reached the summit of *felicitas*: long ago, a Chaldaean seer had told him that he would live to be first among men and die at the height of good fortune. He told the story in his memoirs, not long before his death.[69] Like Marius and the prophecy of his seventh consulship, which seems to have become a driving and ultimately a consuming force in his life; like Caesar and his belief in his fortune; even so Sulla clearly believed the prophecy, especially when it began to work out. Were the signs of illness already upon him?[70] We cannot know. However, we must not ignore or underestimate the irrational motives of men, whether leaders or led, as – in an age of supreme superstition and almost limitless credulity – we still too often take pride in doing. For Sulla, in any case, there was no choice. The care he spent on his system, followed as it was by immediate withdrawal from power in planned stages, shows that he knew it.

Sulla's system basically lasted to the end of the Republic – so we have recently been reminded,[71] with convincing documentation. The old story of the overthrow of the whole system in 70, in the consulship of two of its chief profiteers, had too often lightly been repeated. It was worth stressing how solidly, in many respects, Sulla had built.

Yet the stress on survival can mislead, however useful in righting the balance. No one can deny that the *res publica* of the sixties was vastly different from that of the middle seventies. Perhaps we can now begin to define the difference. Whatever the number of detailed provisions that survived – and they included, among other important parts, the whole of the system of provincial government, perhaps the first such system ever attempted in Rome – these details were all externals. What was altered was the spirit of the system. Let us take an example from the field just mentioned. Sulla had deliberately refrained from annexation and, as we saw, had budgeted for (in principle) an annual change of governor for each province. In the course of the seventies and the sixties, four new provinces were created, added to the ten that Sulla had left;[72] yet no more magistrates were appointed. That change, surely, is more than merely quantitative. And this in addition to the aspects that have always been stressed, though their importance should now be reasserted from the point of view of our conclusions about the spirit of Sulla's work: the revival of the tribunate in the course of the seventies, and the reforms of 70 which completed it and recalled the equites to a share – the major share – in the courts and hence to renewed political power.[73] Balance had again taken the place of central control; the Senate was again only one group of players in the game; the *res publica* that had broken down for lack of *concordia* and that had been replaced by Sulla's radical reform was now restored, with *concordia* no nearer. Those who put the end of the Sullan system in 70 were perhaps, after all, only technically wrong. The French Revolution may perhaps in a very proper sense be said to have been killed by Napoleon (if not before), although many of its organizational details survive to our own day.

But why did the Sullan system fail? We all know that 'Sulla could not abolish his own example'.[74] Pompey, his disciple (as Sallust calls him), at once applied his technique against Sulla himself – and got away with it, with no more than a joke against him. Yet, important though this is, it is not the whole explanation. As has been rightly stressed,[75] Sulla's example also did much to *prevent* real imitation – and indeed, we have seen that this may have been in his mind. The horror of proscription hovers over Roman politics for a generation, constraining ambition and political feud. Pompey, the disciple, was no Sulla in the end (whatever Cicero at one time thought, in despair).[76] And Caesar, who could no longer understand Sulla, while imitating his technique carefully avoided the horrors so well remembered. When civil war came, Sulla's example helped to alleviate its horror, as for a long time it had postponed its coming. We must remember that it was men who had been children in 82 who forced war on Caesar and Pompey in 49;[77] not to mention those who, a few years later, brought back proscription to a city that had forgotten it.

It is hazardous to speak about the basic cause of a complex phenomenon. But if ever it was justified, perhaps this is the case. At least, there is an obvious cause that must by no means be neglected; though it has tended to be, in an age that looks for historical causes in rather a narrow range. Sulla's system failed because he had overrated the oligarchy to which he had entrusted his *res publica*. For one thing, the adlection of the leaders of the irresponsible equites into the weakened Senate held out little hope of improvement. By 70, corruption in the senatorial law-courts was so blatant that even eminent senators agreed it must be reformed[78] – not (one is tempted to say) from any serious hope of improvement, but at least so as to remove it from the sphere of political agitation. This must have been one of the aims of the reform of 70. And it was achieved. Corruption remained, perhaps worse than ever;[79] but responsibility was now shared, and the courts were never again a major political issue. However, corruption was not the worst element. The Empire later survived a good deal of it, as other empires have. Honesty in positions of power has far more often been an ideal, or a pretence, than a fact. The worst was that the oligarchy had lost the will and the confidence to govern. When two *Sullani* (as we saw) destroyed the spirit of the Sullan settlement in 70, there was little real resistance.[80] In fact, the myth of Sulla as restorer and patron soon wore thin. Yet there was no willingness to give up the profits – perhaps no politically easy way of doing so without great risks. Sulla had left a legacy of guilt, from which the better elements among his successors found no escape. The Sullan oligarchy had a fatal flaw: it governed with a guilty conscience.

It was not the only flaw. The post-Sullan oligarchy had no sense of mission. Even outside the selfish ambitions of the men who finally tore it apart, this can be demonstrated. Between 78 and 59, when ordered government may be said to have ceased, twenty-one consuls (over half) are not attested in provincial government. Of course, our records are far from complete, and some will have done their duty without our being aware of it. Others will have been genuinely prevented.[81] Yet surely not over half. There were men who did not want to leave the excitement of the city, or the pleasures of their villas, for the duties of service abroad. We all know Cicero's disgust when, in 52, the Senate exerted pressure on men like him to make them at last face their responsibilities. And although here we are even less well informed, we can be sure that there were praetors too who felt and acted like this. Yet these were among the best of the rulers. They had no hopes of actual gain from provincial government. The effect was a kind of Gresham's law: the bad governors drove out the good. Every Hortensius or Cicero or Bibulus gave a year to a Verres or a Catiline – not to mention a Caesar. A century earlier, religious obstacles had to be affirmed on oath if the aristocrat's burden was to be avoided.[82] This is the measure of the decline. Again, we note the unexpected consequences of reform. Sulla, looking at his own time and his own career, had seen it as his duty to provide against excessive ambition, against over-eagerness to command armies and govern provinces. He had apparently failed to think of inertia and irresponsibility.[83] Yet it was these petty vices that helped to ruin his system.

However, if the oligarchy was not fit to perform the task that Sulla had allotted to it, he himself must take a large share of the blame. There were many signs of danger before, especially in the generation since the tribunate of Tiberius Gracchus. No one can say that Sulla alone caused the decline of senatorial government. But that he greatly accelerated it and gave it a totally new impetus cannot be seriously doubted. When he took a private army against Rome in 88, no one of any importance followed him: the leading citizens disapproved, and Sulla, in the end, had to come to terms. In 87, the decline becomes visible: it was difficult to give up the benefits conferred by the methods of which one disapproved, and most of those same leaders decided to defend their political gains, however brought about. But the end was not yet. Cinna saw what was happening, tried to remedy it, and (as we saw) almost succeeded. Then came his failure, and Sulla's second intervention. And where the effects of the first had been alarming, those of the second were fatal. The vast majority of the ruling class flocked to acclaim the victorious rebel as a saviour, and it became clear that the Republic, for them, was merely a pretext for their own privilege. Those who did not share this attitude – men as different as the Patrician consul L. Scipio Asiagenus and the Sabine new man Q. Sertorius – were mercilessly weeded out. Sulla's new state was based on an absurd parody of natural selection – the survival of the unfittest.

The harm, of course, was not limited to the governing class. In 83-2, many thousands of Italians had rallied to the Republic which had been slow enough in giving them their citizen rights,[84] and had fought Sulla every inch of the way for its sake. Again, the best of them were eliminated, by massacre or exile. It is not difficult to imagine what ordinary men in Italy thought of their betters, who claimed the divine right to rule them and who now flocked to the victorious adventurer, to profit by his success. As for the next generation, we need not even imagine: we know. Thirty years later, much to Cicero's chagrin,[85] the honourable citizens of the Italian towns and countryside would not stir a finger, even on behalf of their own patrons, to defend the *res publica* that had punished their fathers for defending it, or rewarded them for deserting it. Even more than Sulla's example, it was the example of the *Sullani* that could not be abolished. Sulla's well-planned scheme of reform had handed the government over to a class of proved cowards and open self-seekers, who could neither develop confidence in themselves nor inspire it in the governed, neither give up their gains nor show themselves worthy of them. The Republic had begun to putrefy a generation before it died.[86]

1. It might be mentioned that this Lecture was delivered not long after the announcement of the death of Ho Chi Minh and the consequent laudations.

2. I showed this in the paper now in my *Studies in Greek and Roman History*, 1964 (henceforth *Studies*) 208f. The only objection raised (Candiloro, *SCO* 1963, 224 f.; repeated Balsdon, *JRS* 1965, 231) is (I think) demolished *Athenaeum* 1964, 422f. (not yet known to Balsdon).

3. The date can be deduced from the fact that he stood for the praetorship in 99, for 98 (*see* below). The sources (collected *RE*, s.v. 'Cornelius' no. 392) offer the usual vagueness due to ambiguity in the use of ordinal or cardinal numbers in stating ages. Most of the

evidence is collected in *RE*, l.c. and will not be cited here, except where the details are particularly important or controversial.

4. Fragments of the work in Peter, *HRR* i^2 195f.; useful discussion CCLXXf. Fr. 2, mentioning the *flamen Dialis* (of about the middle of the third century), is quoted from Book ii.

5. A favourite story in moralists. *See RE*, s.v. 'Cornelius,' col. 1423.

6. On the family, *see RE*, s.v. 'Cornelius,' coll. 1513f. The taboos of the priest of Jupiter will be found in any handbook, e.g. Wissowa, *Rel. u. Kultus d. Römer*^{2} 102.

7. Best known, perhaps, the Murenae (Cic. *Mur.* 15f.); but examples are easy to find. (Note the Tremellii, Varro, *De Re Rust.* 2.4.2. – seven generations of praetors.)

8. Sall. *Jug.* 95.3 states what we could in any case deduce.

9. Fr. 1 (p. 185) P.

10. Plutarch usually does give the mother's name. The only cases, among his late Republican subjects, where he does not, are those of Pompey and Crassus. We do not know why – perhaps lack of distinction? – Pompey's mother is unknown. Crassus' mother was a Venuleia, as we happen to know (Cic. *Att.* 12.24.2: the textual variant 'Vinuleia' is hardly worth considering, since the Venuleii attain at least moderate prominence). The mothers of Marius and Cicero, perhaps surprisingly, are mentioned. There, presumably, lack of distinction was of the essence of the biography. If so, this ought to apply to Sulla, whose poor beginnings are stressed.

11. Sallust, *Jug.* 96, is emphatic: 'rudis et ignarus belli' before his quaestorship. Plutarch certainly knows of no public (civil or military) service before the quaestorship. In theory, liability to service could not be escaped. But it is easy to imagine that well-connected young men could escape it if they tried. However, it would certainly impair their prospect of holding office.

12. Val. Max. 6.9.6., with nice rhetoric: 'usque ad quaesturae suae comitia uitam libidine, uino, ludicrae artis amore inquinatam perduxit.' His election, at the age of thirty, is later than usual: Ti. Gracchus had been quaestor at 25, C. Gracchus (against opposition) at 27. Again, absence of ambition may account for it, or a sudden chance in 108.

13. Plut. *Sulla* 3; Val. Max., l.c. (last note), who gives Marius' supposed reaction.

14. *See* Sallust, n. 11 (above).

15. *See* L. A. Thompson, *PACA* 1962, 17f.

16. On Julia, *see* Suet. Jul. 6 and, for the stemma, *RE*, s.v. 'Iulius,' coll. 183-4. The fact that she had two brothers about to begin political careers was probably important. (*See* my *For. Client.* (1958) 195, 199 and, for the aristocratic support that Marius tried to build up, 200.

17. A *close* family connection would presumably have been noted by someone, and this can hardly be suggested. A less obvious one might well escape mention, like so much similar information.

18. Plut. *Sulla* 4. The scene, presumably, is the one that survives, for us, on the coin later issued by Sulla's son Faustus (Sydenham, *CRR*, no. 879). Once engraved on the signet, we may be certain that it would serve as the model for Sulla's son. Indeed, it may also have served as the model for the sculptures later dedicated by Bocchus (*see* p. 00).

19. Plut., l.c. It would be interesting to know how common it was for quaestorians to serve as legates in another campaign under their former commanders. No other case is known; but we have little evidence on legates, perhaps less on quaestors. Still, Marius' own circumstances are so unusual that we can assume it must have been exceptional.

20. *See Studies* (n. 2 above) 37f.

21. It could be argued that a legate might not do so, but a tribune might, since his appointment was annual. But I am merely concerned to point out that, in view of Catulus' alliance with Marius at this time, the traditional account cannot be true, whatever the legal aspect.

22. For the consuls of those years, *see MRR*. 99 was the year in which the law authorizing Metellus Numidicus' return from exile was passed; 98 the year in which Marius seems to have received his augurate in absence and to have returned from the East in consequence. For the chronology, *see* Gabba's edition of Appian, *Bell. Civ.* 1 (1958), pp. 111, 114f., and (for Marius) *Studies* 171 with notes.

23. *See Studies* 157f., for the first time (as far as I am aware) working out the chronology, and discussing the Cilician proconsulship in detail.

24. 'iners et inimicus fori' (*Br.* 237).

25. *Studies* 34f. Gruen, *Historia* 1966, 32f. offers a long critical commentary on that article, and I am prepared to accept some of his points. But I have found no reason to revise my view on he importance and effects of the trials of the middle nineties. On

Censorinus, Gruen tries to counter my suggestion (*see* text) with a very different one: 'Censorinus may have been cooperating with another Marcius, L. Marcius Philippus' (p. 52). This is surely the sort of mechanistic prosopography that has brought the whole technique into disrepute: no connection between the Censorini and the Philippi (other than the coincidence of *nomen*) is attested, as far as I know, throughout their recorded history. My own suggestion – admittedly only tentative – is at least based on proven collaboration eight years later. Where nothing can be known for certain, rational conjecture (advanced with due caution) is surely preferable to unfounded guesswork.

26. That the hostility between Marius and Catulus was slow to develop is shown by the fact that the Greek poet Archias managed to please both of them (Cic. *Arch.* 5f., 19). But we have no detailed chronological indication.

27. As clearly demonstrated by the omission of the aedileship, which he could well afford.

28. The main sources are collected in Greenidge-Clay[2] 125f.

29. Cic. *ap.* Asc. 21C: 'Cum . . . P. Rutilio damnato nemo tam innocens uideretur ut non timeret illa' [i.e. iudicia]. For the attack on the great M. Scaurus, *see* Greenidge-Clay[2] 127. The tangled evidence is carefully sorted by Gruen, *Roman Politics and the Criminal Courts* (1968) 206, and *op. cit.* (n. 25, above) 55f.

30. This has been discussed innumerable times. For the sources *see MRR* ii 21 f., for my own interpretation *For. Client.* 215f. For the political background of the reforms, *see* Gabba, *ASNP* 1964, 1f.

31. Dio, fr. 97.3. The two men were old *inimici* (*see Studies* 39). For Sulla as protégé of the *factio* against Marius, *see* Plut. *Mar.* 32.

32. The exact chronology cannot be recovered, since we have only Plutarch's account (*Sulla* 6 = *Marius* 32). But it must be late 91. Taken strictly, Plutarch suggests the time after Drusus' death: he says that the city was almost on fire with the dispute between Marius and Sulla, and it was only the actual outbreak of the Social War that put an end to it. Sulla may have been trying to fill the gap left by Drusus' death in the front rank of the *factio*, particularly since the death of M. Scaurus could no doubt already be foreseen. As we shall see, Sulla was, in a sense, the heir of Drusus.

33. Cf. Livy 28.39.18; 43.6.6f.; 45.44.8; *et al.*

34. We must bear in mind, of course, that the number of senators present may have been small: we do not know whether a quorum was required for such occasions, and if so, what was its size. But

official approval must, at any rate, have been given. It would be interesting to know, whether, e.g., the *princeps* M. Scaurus was present.

35. In fact, Appian reports an act of co-operation between them *Bell. Civ.* 1.46: against the Marsi). This cannot be true, as Sulla was not fighting in this area (cf. Gabba *ad loc.*; Salmon, *Samnium and the Samnites* (1967), 352f., especially 355f., where he regards it as deliberate distortion due to Sulla's own account).

36. Cf. the incident noted in Plut. *Sulla* 6.

37. Plutarch (l.c.) citing Livy, relates that many people who had thought him worthy of the consulship did not think him worthy of this marriage. This is the only evidence on the relative order of the two events. It is likely that the actual arrangements for both were made at the same time. As for the marriage of Sulla's daughter to Q. Pompeius, their son was tribune in 52 (*MRR* ii 236). Even if born 87 (the latest date possible, since the father was killed in the riots of 88), he would be rather old for that office. Hence it is likely that the marriage only took place in 89 or 88, although there is no decisive evidence.

38. For the date of this (89, not 88, since at the beginning of Sulpicius' tribunate) *see For. Client.* 230f.; *Historia* 1969, 418f.

39. Sall. *Jug.* 73.7. (The sense of the supplement is certain.)

40. Plut. *Mar.* 35; *Sulla* 8.

41. Sall. *Jug.* 862; Val. Max. 3.3.1; Gell. 16.10.10f. (quoting Sallust). On this step and its importance, *see* Gabba, *Athenaeum* 1951, 171f.

42. App. *Bell. Civ.* 1.57, *Studies* 220.

43. App. *Bell. Civ.* 1.59 (see Gabba's notes *ad loc.*); cf. Gabba, *op.cit.* (n. 30, above) 7f.

44. The elections must not (as they sometimes are) be interpreted as a sign of 'popular disapproval': what is shown by the centuriate assembly is the hostility of the propertied classes. It must be remembered (as I have tried to stress, against the propagandist distortions in some of our sources) that at this time Sulla was the leader of a mercenary army of have-nots: a phenomenon unwelcome to those classes.

45. Sources collected Greenidge-Clay^2 171f. Sulla, clearly, was well in advance of his generation in his precise analysis of the possibilities of the 'client army' – and in his unscrupulous rationality in adapting his actions to them.

46. Plut. *Sulla* 11 contrasts with App. *Mithr.* 29. For a recent

discussion (citing earlier bibliography) *see* M. Janke, *Histor. Unters. zu Memnon v. Herakleia* (Diss. Würzburg, 1963) 53f. Plutarch reports that the legate Q. Braetius (?) Sura defeated the Pontic troops, which had to withdraw to the sea. Appian says that the legate did not face the enemy forces, but withdrew to Piraeus, until Archelaus occupied it. As Janke shows, a notice about these events in Paus. 1.20.5, (a battle in which the Romans defeat Archelaus and drive him back into Piraeus, before the beginning of the siege of Athens) must refer to the same engagement. (No Roman commander is named by Pausanias; Sulla only appears on the scene later. Probably he omitted the unknown and unimportant name he found in his source.) The version in Appian is certainly wrong, since Piraeus was held by Pontic troops and a Roman commander cannot have withdrawn to it; and, had he done so, he could not have retired to Macedonia after. (It was only Sulla who gained control of the sea.) That version is therefore due either to a misunderstanding of the source (perhaps the more likely explanation, and far from unparalleled) or possibly distortion in a pro-Sullan source (Sisenna?) not used by Plutarch. Plutarch's version suggests that Sulla had nothing to the contrary to report in his own account, and should all the more readily be accepted. It confirms Sulla's mastery in assessing the psychology of the client army, the chances it offered and its limitations (*see* n. 45 and text, above).

47. *Studies* (n. 2, above) 222f.

48. *See* especially Plut. *Sulla* 6 and cf. (whatever it means: *see* Balsdon, *JRS* 1951, 1f.) his later *agnomen* 'Felix.'

49. *Studies* 226f., demonstrating the (fairly obvious) purposes of Cinna's Illyrian expedition against the distortion of Sullan sources and its acceptance by scholars unaware of geographical and military realities. (That the latter have not given up is known by Balsdon, *JRS* 1965, 232.)

50. Evidence *Studies* 229f.

51. On Sulla as the new Romulus *see* Alföldi, *MH* 1951, 205f.

52. *See* Gabba, *op.cit.* (n. 30, above).

53. This programme did not disappear with Drusus' failure and death, but remained a live issue in politics. I have tried to trace its vicissitudes and importance in *Historia* 1969, 447f.

54. I have developed this in my De Carle Lectures, delivered at the University of Otago in July-August 1969. (Pulbications forthcoming 1971).

55. For the view that C. Gracchus was thinking of the 'mixed

constitution,' *see* Rowland, *TAPA* 1965, 361f. C. Gracchus was certainly the first Roman who clearly had in mind a comprehensive scheme of reform, so that the question of theoretical influences cannot be lightly dismissed (as it still can, I think, in the case of his brother). But *see* Nicolet, *REA* 1965, 142f.

56. Varro *ap.* Non. Marc. 728 L.

57. App. *Bell. Civ.* 1.21 cf. 34. Appian's account has been questioned, but without reason or counter-evidence. Though this is not, of course, to assert that the problem would not have come up but for the commission's activities.

58. *See Historia*, l.c. (n. 53 above), with recent bibliography.

59. Livy, *Per* 86. Salmon has shown (*Athenaeum* 1964, 60f.) that the Social War did not merge into the civil war on Sulla's return and that there was no simple connection between them: Italy, like Rome, was divided in its allegiance (esp. pp. 68f.). Sulla landed at Brundisium without opposition (App. *Bell. Civ.* 1.79), but, coming up against strong Italian opposition in Campania (based on his cancellation of Sulpicius' laws in 88), in due course 'made a treaty with the Italians' (Livy, l.c.) committing himself to recognize their rights. Salmon suggests that the Samnites were excluded from the treaty, possibly because they objected to some aspects of its terms. (I see no evidence for his further conjecture that 'they had no part in the treaty simply because Sulla had already made up his mind to keep them out' (*op.cit.* 75).) In support of this, one might compare their attitude to the original grant of citizenship by the *lex Julia*: they had stood out for special terms, implying total Roman surrender, and had in the end won them. (*See* App. *Bell. Civ.* 1.68; Gran. Lic. 20 F; the terms in Dio, fr. 102.7.)

60. On the Samnites, cf. Strabo 5.4.11; for Italy, e.g., Flor. 2.9.27, and *see* passages collected Greenidge-Clay^2 216f.; Cic. *Caec.* 97 (Arretium), *dom.* 79 (Volaterrae).

61. *See* n. 52 and text (above). For Crassus' young disciples, *see* Cic. *De Or.* 1.24f. Perhaps Crassus' *magistra oratio* in support of Caepio's law in 106 foreshadows some such ideas (*see* Cic. *De Or.* 1.225); and cf. *Historia* 1969, *cit.* (n. 53, above).

62. Evidence collected Greenidge-Clay^2 213f. Cf. Mommsen, *Röm. Staatsr.* ii^3 200f.

63. The privilege was 'restored' by law of L. Roscius Otho in 67 (Cic. *Mur.* 40) – which is further evidence for the slowness of the equites' restoration to power and privilege. Otho's law is clearly a consequence of their return to the juries in 70, which itself was

probably not due to any pressure on their part.

64. This is not the place to enter into the discussion (raised by Nicolet's great work) on the definition of the *ordo equester* in the late Republic. I am here using the word 'equites' as it was undoubtedly used by Cicero. On the adlection to the Senate, *see* Gabba, *Athenaeum* 1956, 124f.; Hawthorn, *G. & R.* 1962, 53f. Those chosen were not confined to the 18 centuries.

65. App. *Bell. Civ.* 1.95 puts the number of equites proscribed at 1600. *See* Gabba's note *ad loc.* (pp. 254f.). Other sources appear to confirm some such figure.

66. That this practice had developed during the preceding generation, largely owing to the multiplication of judicial business and jury ćourts, is clear from our detailed evidence (easily consluted in *MRR*) and obvious on mere arithmetical grrounds. *See* Mommsen, *Röm. Staastr. cit.* (n. 62, above).

67. I tentatively worked out the 'time-table' of Sulla's retirement *Historia* 1962, 230f. and have given further details in a forthcoming article in *Athenaeum* (publication promised for 1970).

68. Or perhaps *pretended* he could not: 'nihil esse rem publicam, appellationem modo sine corpore ac specie; Sullam nescisse litteras, qui dictaturam deposuerit' (Suet. *Jul.* 77). The source is T. Ampius Balbus, not a sound witness, but there are reasons for believing him here (Syme, *Roman Revolution*, 1939, 53).

69. Plut. *Sulla* 27. This was when, in his province after his praetorship, he met an embassy from the King of Parthia (*ibid* 5). Compare the omen that promised Marius seven consulships and that seems to have been a motivating force in his efforts to return to prominence in and after the late nineties. (For the omen *see* Plut. *Mar.* 36; App. *Bell. Civ.* 1.61; 75. It is not mentioned in recent accounts of Marius.) Compare also the fatal trust of Cn. Octavius (*cos.* 87) in soothsayers and astrologers (Plut. *Mar.* 42; App. *Bell. Civ.* 1.71). This *motiv* should often be taken much more seriously than it nowadays is.

70. For an interesting discussion of his illness and death, implying that he could indeed have known some time in advance, *see* Carney, *AClass* 1960, 64f.

71. In an interesting study by U. Laffi (a pupil of Gabba), 'Il mito di Silla,' *Athenaeum* 1967, 177f., 255f. *See* especially part I, section 2 (pp. 179f.).

72. For the ten provinces under Sulla, *see* Mommsen, *Röm. Staatsr.* ii^3 201. After Sulla, Cyrene was organized provisionally in

74, permanently perhaps only by Pompey; Bithynia-Pontus and Syria by Pompey; and Crete by Q. Metellus Creticus or Pompey; (details are not known). Cyprus was added in 58/7, but joined to Cilicia.

73. For the politics of the seventies, *see* the interesting discussion by R. Rossi, *PP* 1965, 133f. For the removal of the limitations on the tribunate, *see* the sources collected Greenidge-Clay^2 245, 250, 256. One might add (though it is not a constitutional measure) Cn. Lentulus' law of 72, cancelling the remissions of payment for the estates of the proscribed, which Sulla had granted (Sall. *Hist.* 4.1 M). For the reforms of 70, *see* sources collected Greenidge-Clay^2 270f. Whatever the definition of the *tribuni aerarii*, who provided the third panel of jurors after that year, Cicero usually regards their interests as identical with those of the equites.

74. Syme, *Rom. Rev.* 17.

75. Laffi, *op,cit.* (n. 71, above).

76. Laffi, *op.cit.* 268f. (based on Syme, *op.cit.* 65) discusses the propaganda war of the late fifties and the forties that depicted Pompey as a new Sulla. (For Cicero's attitude, *see* 271f.)

77. The 'rash and factious minority' (Syme, *op.cit.* 47) has been brilliantly delineated and analysed by Syme. Of the consulars later on Pompey's side, the oldest, L. Afranius (*cos.* 60 as a middle-aged *nouus homo*), born probably before 110, was away in Spain during the long debate on Caesar's *imperium*; the next oldest, M. Bibulus, was governing Syria. (Cicero, slightly older, was, of course, not only away from Rome, but vigorously opposed to the decision for war.) The oldest actually in Rome was P. Lentulus Spinther, who triumphed late in 51: as *cos.* 57, he must have been born in 100 at the latest and may have been a little earlier. But although a loyal partisan when the time came, he is not reported as active in the debates. L. Ahenobarbus (*cos.* 54, after a year's delay) was therefore the oldest active enemy of Caesar. He was born in 98, we may assume, Ap. Claudius (also *cos.* 54) in 97; M. Cato (never consul, but one of the moving spirits in the fight against Caesar) in 95. The consul C. Marcellus who, late in 50, handed Pompey a sword after ignominiously failing to rally the Senate to his cause, probably had had a regular *cursus* (aedile 56) and was born in 93. No one active against Caesar in 50-49, therefore, was over sixteen years old when Sulla was made dictator.

78. Cicero makes this clear in the *Verrines*, e.g. 1. *Verr.* 44.

79. The acquittal of Clodius is only the most famous of many

scandals.

80. For the view of Catulus, *see* Cicero, l.c. (n. 78, above). It was the family of the Cottae, *ex factione media*, that was responsible for the partial abrogation of Sulla's law on the tribunate and for the judicial law of 70 (Sall. *Hist.* 3.48.8 M; cf. Asc. 78 C; Greenidge-Clay[2] 272f.) *See also* Rossi, *op.cit.* (n. 73, above).

81. I append my list. Certain or reasonably certain cases are marked*. *Q. Catulus (78) (fought, briefly, against M. Lepidus); D. Brutus (77); Cn. Octavius (76); *L. Gellius Publicola, *Cn. Lentulus Clodianus (72); *P. Lentulus Sura, Cn. Aufidius Orestes (71); *Cn. Pompeius, *M. Crassus (70); *Q. Hortensius (69); (*L. Metellus (68: died in office)); M. Lepidus, L. Volcacius Tullus (66); *L. Cotta (65); *L. Caesar, *C. Marcius Figulus (64); *M. Cicero (63); D. Silanus, L. Murena (62); M. Piso, *M. Messalla (Niger) (61); (*Q. Metellus Celer (60; perhaps died before he could go)); *M. Bibulus (59). On praetors we are less well informed; but the case of the jurist Ser. Sulpicius Rufus (Cic. *Mur.* 42), plus Cicero's own, cannot leave any doubt that praetors were free to refuse and that some did. The *SC* quoted by Caelius in 51 (Cic. *Fam.* 8.8.8) suggests that a fair supply of such men was available at that time.

82. Livy 41.15.10f. (176 BC). In the same year, another praetor was excused for clear reasons of public policy (*ibid* s.6). The formal reason for the change in practice was presumably that by the first century each praetor had already had a *prouincia* in the city and could claim that he was not liable to serve again *ex praetura*. Nevertheless, the change in spirit invites comment.

83. Pompey's law of 52, reforming provincial administration on the basis of a *SC* of the previous year, also seems to have avoided compulsion; but the Senate expressed strong views, which could not reasonably be resisted. (*See* Cic. *Fam.* 15.4.4: 'quod ego negotium [his provincial command]. . . . uerecundia deterritus non recusaui; neque enim umquam ullum periculum tantum putaui quod subterfugere mallem quam uestrae auctoritati obtemperare.') In the *SC* of 51 (Cic. *Fam.* 8.8.8), the language seems to brook no disobedience.

84. Only, it seems, after Cinna's policy of compromise and conciliation (of his political opponents, at the Italians' expense) had failed: Livy, *Per.* 84 (84 BC).

85. E.g. *Att.* 7.13a.2; 8.13.2; *et al.*

On Reading a Horatian Satire

An Interpretation of Sermones *2.6*

C. O. BRINK

Professor Todd was on the staff of the Department of Latin from 1903 to 1944 – 41 years, for nearly half of which he presided over its affairs. His high scholarly standards and his devotion to the cause of Classics in this University impose an obligation on any Todd Memorial Lecturer which it is not easy to discharge. I am grateful for the honour of this invitation.

In the last half-century or so, when Professor Todd here fostered the classical tradition, a new manner of looking at literature has grown up, and now stands in full vigour. This manner is not only independent of the classical tradition, but owes its very existence to a different set of judgements, or prejudices. These were developed in converse with literatures in living languages. Whatever metaphors are now employed, to describe the poetic process, the 'form' or 'sytle' of a poem will be felt to be inseparably interwoven with its 'subject.' This is far away from the ancient kind of poetry, which talked about man and the world in pre-existing genres and in styles suitable to those genres, so that originality lay in enlivening a traditional form.

The question then arises: do we rightly continue to read ancient poetry as many used to, on the basis of the ancient literary tradition? If we do, can we hope to respond to ancient poetry with personal vigour and subtlety? But if we do not, and approach ancient poetry with our, that is, modern, assumptions, do we not introduce a strange and unrelated note into the Graeco-Roman poetic world?

Horatian satire is a case in point. How are we to read that kind of verse? It is not often satire – or what we commonly mean by the word. Is is poetry? Horace occasionally says not, yet strenuously practises it; some modern readers say it is. What does Horace mean to do with it? What can we do with it?

* * *

Let us use, as a test case, one of the best, perhaps the best, of these poems, the sixth of the Second Book of the *Satires* – *Hoc erat in uotis.*

It begins with Horace speaking apparently in one of his most intimate and self-revealing moods. He has been praying for a farm – not too large, with a garden, a spring of everflowing water by the house, and a small piece of woodland.[1] 'Small' is the keynote – *non ita magnus* and *paulum siluae.*[2] Horace did not crave much. And not craving much he earned contentment when he was given what he prayed for, and a little more. Apparently the gods did that for him, *auctius atque/di melius fecere*[3] is the answer to the former prayer, *hoc erat in uotis.* The god in particular responsible is, not unreasonably, the god of gain and good luck, Mercury, whom he then addresses, *Maia nate.*[4] Mercury, however, people do not normally pray to when they want sufficiency; they pray to him when they want as much as possible: this additional corner of land

and that pot of money. Not so the farmer-poet Horace. His new prayer is, Mercury, make fat the flocks and other possessions that I have but keep my mind lean.[5]

This, it seems, is protesting too much. The mood of contentment – *bene est*[6] – is that of a real person. But then, in front of our very eyes, Horace turns himself into a philosophical case – the wise man, content with little. Having been put on our guard, perhaps we want to know: how literally may we take Horace the farmer, the countryman?

'So (he goes on) having withdrawn from the city to my hilly stronghold, what should I rather celebrate in the prose poetry of satire? Here neither sordid jostling for position upsets me' nor the evil climate of the city.[7] So the passage closes and we expect to hear the praises of the country sung by the countryman – something of the order of what the poet's ancient commentator, Porphyrion, naively found in this satire: the poet 'praises the country and displays its freedom from care,' *laudat rus et securitatem eius exponit*. But that is precisely what we do not hear. Instead a different person appears on the stage – Horace the townsman. He sings no praises. The serene and sincere note of contentment has faded out. A racy realism takes its place – a satire on life in the city, with Horace as its butt. Mercury too is gone; the presiding godhead is the Father of the early morning, *Matutinus Pater*, or Janus, the god of beginnings.[8]

For Janus stirs him out of the house in the early morning to act as a surety: 'up with you' – *heia* – get a move on, make sure that no one meets the call of duty before you, *officio . . . respondeat*.[9] And so, whatever the weather – 'the outing is inescapable,' *ire necesse est*.[10] Then the declaration, which may harm him financially, in the streets the battle with the crowds, to shove and be shoved, and to listen to angry protests, 'you would push anything out of your way and think of no one else when you are hurrying back to Maecenas.'[11] Here then is the name which is at the bottom of it all, Maecenas. The person thus accosting him maliciously implies that when Horace is in a hurry it is because he is on his way back to his patron. The poet does not seem to mind the innuendo. Indeed he deliberately says: *hoc iuuat et melli est, non mentiar*, 'to be honest, this is pleasing and sweet as honey.'[12] But he pays for his pleasure. The closer he gets to the great man's house, the more *aliena negotia*, 'other people's affairs,' press in on him.[13] A law suit, a discussion by the guild of clerks, *scribae*, to which he still seems to have belonged; a request for an urgent sealing by Maecenas: such are the obstacles on the way.

It is only when one reads on that one begins to realize that even this honeyed pleasure is not honey unmixed. For so far from taking us to Maecenas' house, he becomes autobiographical. Horace has been a member of Maeceans' circle for nearly eight years; but what do they discuss when they drive out together? The hour of the day, sport, the weather. What does he get in return? Envy all round for being in on secrets of state; requests for information that he has not got; incredulity when he has to plead ignorance.[14]

No wonder, then, the country comes back into view. Yet what was a prayer realized at the outset – *hoc erat in uotis*, the poem began, and *bene est* – is now, when he recalls it, nostalgia. 'So this day is wasted in wretchedness, not without a prayer' – *non sine uotis*[15] recalling the first verse, *hoc erat in uotis* –, 'o country when shall I see you?' *o rus, quando ego te aspiciam?*[16] The country, his books, sleep and leisure, a forgetting of a life of troubles – all this is now a wish unfulfilled: he has it, yet he has it not.

It is here that the last part of the poem begins. A vision

of the peace of the country appears to a troubled townsman; civilization yearns for simplicity; busy meddling yearns for simple-mindedness. This note of yearning is beautifully resolved in the fairly-tale atmosphere that now supervenes – a state of bliss in which human personality is at one with itself. 'O divine nights and dinners,' *o noctes cenaeque deum.*[17] It is country fare, sparingly eaten; drinks large or small offered as one may like; the setting is Horace's own home, *ante Larem proprium* (not other people's houses), and the diners are 'he and his,' *ipse meique* (not the people he must meet in Rome).[18] What matters is conversation, *ergo sermo oritur*; the subject, not the talk of busybodies concerning house property and the style of ballet stars, but 'what concerns us more nearly' and ignorance of which is harmful, *malum est.*[19] And then there follow the kinds of topic which Graeco-Roman moral theory liked to discuss. Does happiness rest on wealth or goodness? Does friendship rest on expediency or morality? What is the highest good?[20] This sort of talk could be ponderous and utterly out of keeping with the rest of the poem. It is a measure of Horace's art that few things sound more natural than these seminars on moral philosophy at the poet's *cenae deum*. Perhaps no device could be more successful than that adopted by him. He places an animal fable at the end, told with great dramatic vigour and such relish and attention to detail that one forgets its length – nearly 40 verses, one third of the satire.[21] If moral theory can put up with a fable, then the theory obviously fits a true conversation; Horace is not after all conducting seminars. The teller of the tale serves the same purpose. He is one Cervius, a rustic neighbour of the poet, who would not be likely to attend a seminar.

Cervius prattles away between whiles telling stories that suit the case, *anilis/ex re fabellas*.[22] How they are *ex re* can be seen at once. One of the guests has expressed admiration for a wealthy man, Arellius, without being aware of the anxieties wealth causes.[23] So this is a living example of the topic, 'is human happiness caused by wealth or goodness?'[24] The fable of the town mouse and the country mouse is a cautionary tale; Horace's art is flexible enough to accommodate such a tale along with subjects on a very different level of sophistication. It is simple as all fables are. The country mouse is persuaded by its friend to accompany him to the city, where he is offered a civilized dinner in civilized surroundings. Suddenly a terrible banging of doors and a barking of large hounds send them tumbling. The country man, or mouse (he is just *rusticus*), speaks the epilogue, 'This sort of life I have no use for – and so farewell,' *haud mihi vita est opus hac, ait, et ualeas*; 'my wood and hole will console me with simple vetch, safe as it is from ambushes' – *tutus ab insidiis*. The tale seems unsophisticated but its use in the poem is not.

What does the poem add up to? If the question is so put, the answer must be, 'nothing.' A poem does not add up to anything that can be stated as a sum total in conceptual terms. In this regard a poem is like a piece of music – it evolves in time, as a time sequence. You 'have' the poem if you follow it as it evolves, although you may look back on it from various points of vantage; and no Horatian poem can be understood if the reader does not keep looking back from unexpected points of vantage.

What strikes me first is, how complex that seeming unity really is, and how full of contradictions – a true picture of human motivation. First take Horace the countryman. The feeling of contentment, *bene est*, at the beginning, is quite genuine. And we may even condone, because Horace condones it humorously, that he has now become the model of a contented sage. But the reader is pulled up sharply when the solemn introduction does not lead to a praise of the country, but instead there appears Horace the townsman. Moreover life in Rome is not all obnoxious. The antithesis that is offered is not town v. country, or not only that. For it has escaped no attentive reader that Horace likes life in Rome, however irritating some of its corollaries. The setting is highly artificial and selective. Maecenas was not the only person in Rome whose company Horace enjoyed, although, for reasons that will soon appear, the poem is tied to the person of his friend and patron. Nor does Horace hint only at friends. Shouldering his way through the crowds he is told angrily, 'you would push anything out of your way and think of no one else when you are hurrying back to Maecenas.'[25] He remarks, *hoc iuuat et melli est, non mentiar*;[26] and commentators cannot make up their minds whether this means, 'I enjoy hurrying back to Maecenas' or 'I enjoy being recognized as the great man's friend.' I find the latter harder to believe than the former. In any case, it is hard to overlook the pleasure implied in the close contact with Maecenas, which generates so much envy, and the palpable irony that prompts the specimens of his talk with his friend. If these two had nothing to talk about but the hour of day, the weather, and sport, Horace would not have been Horace, and Maecenas would hardly have been Maecenas.

I believe then that the black and white antithesis, city-country, is convincing only on the surface. Horace is a townsman and his love for the country is that of a townsman.[27] To make this real Horace had to make real what detains and, in a sense, pleases him in his life in Rome. Otherwise the picture would have been unconvincing To make it a poetic protrait he has set a central piece, 'Horace the townsman,' in a sharply contrasted framework, 'Horace the countryman.' If the poem only consisted of the *bene est* of the beginning and the *cenae deum* of the end, the countryman would not have been a man of mind, taste, and civilization. It is the central piece, with its 'on the one hand' and 'on the other hand,' which lends sense and verisimilitude to the *cena* at the end. And conversely this explains why Horace breaks off after his introduction although we expect him there to begin his praise of the country. Horace the countryman starts the poem; the townsman takes over; and the countryman ends it – only he has changed some of his features.

Horace had a sense of the different values inherent in town and country, and felt the pull of each. He got poetic capital out of the antithesis in different ways. In the 2nd Epode he does it by a simple *coup*. A person undefined celebrates for 66 verses the innocent and carefree ways of country life – *beatus ille qui procul negotiis*[28] –, but the poet discloses in the last four that the speaker is the financier Alfius, on the verge of a large financial operation. The 10th Epistle of the first book is a confrontation of an *urbis amator* with the *ruris amator*, Horace; the 14th a humorous dialectic comparison between Horace, who longs for the country, and his bailiff, who longs for Rome. The fault lies in their minds which cannot escape from themselves, *in culpa est animus qui se non effugit umquam*.[29] Similar antitheses are found in other poems. In our poem both the contrary aspects are aspects of Horace's mind. In the satire following ours in Book ii the poet caricatures this by allowing one of his slaves to list this among his master's many faults – 'at Rome you wish for the country; in the country, in your fickleness, you praise the distant city to the skies'.[30] It shows the stature of our poem that it accommodates the two aspects without caricature and commonplace.

There is another contradiction, both logical and psychological, which Horace exploits for poetic purposes – I mean his indebtedness to Maecenas. Commentators have always taken it for granted that this satire is a tactful and delicate way of expressing the poet's thanks to his patron for the gift of the Sabine farm. Now in a sense it is – to anyone who happens to know the identity of the donor. For Horace does not here so much as allude to it; the donor, so far as it goes, is Mercury. The recipient does not allow himself even the hint of one of the *Odes* in Book ii, 'I importune the gods for nothing beyond this, nor do I crave more from my powerful friend; the wealth of *one* Sabine farm is sufficient.'[31]

This reticence however enables him to be frank in a different way. For I should have thought the poem makes it quite clear that, since Maecenas was the donor, Horace is indebted to him not only for his countryman's existence but also for his townsman's existence, which is as much the basis as it is the negation of the other. Indeed if one took him at his word, he should have been full of longing for the unknown and unattached existence which he led in Rome before he became a member of Maecenas' circle. But that would be a literal and flat-footed reading. The 6th satire of Book i puts it beyond doubt that to be unattached was part of the good life to Horace's mind; this coloured his view of his life in the city at an earlier period when he was poor and unknown, just as it now colours his view of life in the country. To Horace the man these strains and stresses may have been an occasional embarrassment. To Horace the poet they offered a chance, which he took, of adding a new complexity to his poetry. Perhaps it will be seen now that if other reasons had not debarred him from addressing to the donor a poem of thanks for the Sabine farm, motives of workmanship might have done so. Otherwise he could not have written the poem as we have it.

No better name than 'moral dialectic' occurs to me for the way in which the poet has shaped his material. It is not the dialectic of the philosophers, yet it is a strongly rational principle. Two pairs of logical opposites or contradictions are made to serve this purpose. One pair is dominant, the other is subordinate. The dominant pair is Horace the countryman: Horace the townsman. The countryman provides the framework: Horace begins with the country, and returns to it in a circle at the end. The city forms the centre of the poem, surrounded by its antithesis. The subordinate pair is Horace's indebtedness to Maecenas for his countryman's existence and Horace's indebtedness to Maecenas for his townsman's existence – the former only implied, as we have seen, but so forcibly implied that no one to my knowledge has ever doubted it; the latter explicit.

I have said that Horace's moral dialectic is not that of the philosophers. Yet it is closer to it than to autobiography. There are people who take Horace literally, and think that he tells us something about his person. They are mistaken. He only *seems* to talk about Horace the individual. For, as we have seen, the traits which he discloses are so selective, so sharply overstated or typified, that in fact we learn very little about himself, though we may learn something about ourselves and the world, if we wish to. While his voice remains unmistakable, his person disappears behind his poetry, and changes from poem to poem. He knows how to make himself into a plurality of egos, a series of contrasting types, and he holds those contrasts in a humorous-ironic balance. This apparent autobiography has a purpose. Horace has a great measure of impersonality and a dramatic gift. He is neither a townsman nor a countryman nor his patron's man nor a courtier nor a lover; he is, in his best work, a poet using typical human attitudes to feel, understand, control the poetic complexity of life. He who seeks in poetry the force of *one* single attitude, *one* powerful emotion, will not find this poet his poet.

In the present poem the complex of motifs, and of ways of expressing them, is fairly large. Let us see how it is controlled by that moral positioning which I have described.

Our satire has a pretty large measure of realism both in description and conversation. It purports to make poetry out of life as it is lived and out of the motives of those that live it. Its style mirrors that purpose. The tempo of city life is fast and this account of it gives the same impression of breathless haste which the poet maintains it gives him. It is a remarkable feat of craftsmanship that the stately hexameter verse can be so speeded up without losing its rhythmic pattern. Horace is snatched away on financial business as soon as he leaves his house. He has to shoulder his way through the crowds. He is overwhelmed by chores pressing in on him from all sides. He cannot escape urgent calls from the many who believe that he has access to all the state secrets.

Conversation too matches for rapidity and variability the talk of Roman comedy. Yet it is beautifully adapted to what the hexameter line can take. 'Up with you, get a move on, make sure that no one meets the call of duty before you', *heia,/ ne prior officio quiaquam respondeat, urge.*[32]'What's on your mind, you lunatic, what are you trying to do?': *quid tibi uis, insane, et quam rem agis?*[33] ' "Get Maecenas, if you please, to put his seal on these papers." If one answers, 'I'll try,' he adds, 'if you will you can,' and insists,' '*imprimat his cura, Maecenas signa tabellis.' / dixeris, 'experiar;' 'si uis potes,' addit et instat.*[34] Polite dialogue is no less flexible, as the passage on state secrets demonstrates amusingly.

The party at the Sabine farm has the same life-likeness. But its tempo and character are just the opposite. Now all is leisurely and happy and homely, down to the dinner of beans, 'the relations of Pythagoras,'[35] and 'the tender garden greens well dressed with fat bacon,' *uncta satis pingui . . . holuscula lardo.*[36] The feeling of contentment, of freedom to attend to the things that really matter, is caught so well that the conjunction of sophisticated moral theory – 'the nature of goodness and its highest form' – with the animal fable, contributed by the rustic neighbour, seems the most natural thing in the world.

The fable itself – a masterpiece of dramatic narrative – repeats in the small world of animals what has previously been performed on the larger, human, stage. It clinches the matter with a moral, the country mouse saying, 'I have no use for that sort of life; so farewell.'[37] Horace's flexibility is such that the moral may clinch the matter of the narrative but does not settle the poet's 'case.' For he is not saying good-bye to all that, to live in safety ever thereafter.

Yet the same realistic style can rise without strain to considerable seriousness and intensity. I do not mean the mock-heroic highlights, which now and again add a touch of parody to the narrative. I mean such a thing as the prayer that opens the poem. 'This was the burden of my prayer,' *hoc erat in uotis*. 'More and better the gods have done. It is well. No greater thing I ask, Son of Maia; only make these gifts last,' *auctius atque/di melius fecere. bene est. nil amplius oro,/Maia nate, nisi ut propria haec mihi munera faxis.*[38]

The whole fabric of the poem is shot with this personal skein. But its colour is ever-changing. At the outset it is the poet's contentment. Then a rapid and surprising change – an emotion mixed of dissatisfaction and pleasure with what after all is inseparably tied to his good fortune: city life. And we understand why he makes us return with him to an even more intense feeling of relief in the final part of the poem – happiness with what is simple and right. This he finds in the country and in the sanity of its people, who are as far removed from the discontents of civilization as Horace is not. The rustic neighbour thus becomes an ideal figure and the animal fable an *exemplum* of moral choice.

Wordsworth in his letter to Christopher North demanded that poets should look out of themselves to men 'who lead the simplest lives, and those most according to nature; men who have never known false refinements, wayward and artificial desires, false criticism,' etc. Generally, he notes, we associate with 'gentlemen, persons of fortune, professional men, ladies.' 'Few descend lower, among cottages and fields, and among children.'[39] The conclusion of our satire seems to suggest that Horace's *Sabinum* pointed the same moral. But it also suggests that Wordsworth took his cultural primitivism more literally than Horace would have done. Horace is not what Shelley called Wordsworth, 'a solemn man.' There is admiration but also an affectionate smile on Horace's features when he talks of the country. Although neighbour Cervius' tale is the note on which the poem closes, it is introduced by the significant words, 'he prattles away, telling stories that suit the case,' *garrit anilis/ex re fabellas.*[40] Both these things are true for the maker of this satire – the stories and their suitability to the case.

Here then is a poet who, in the same poem, takes for his province widely separated fields of experience and reality. In his best work (to which the present one belongs) he can make us view them as separate and united. Diversity is perhaps the first impression on reading a Horatian poem. There are the sharp edges, the abrupt changes of matter and mood, which remind one of some of the poetry written in our century. Of these changes the present poem offers some notable examples. The variability of tone, the complexity of his motifs even in shortish poems, make their reading a bracing and exhilarating experience.

But, just as strongly marked, there is an overall unity.

That is what I called the ironic balance which Horace strikes between the contradictory claims that are made on him – a moral and rational problem turned into a poetic. The *Hoc erat in uotis* is an outstanding personal poem in which a few simple dialectic contradictions are used to keep a grip on a complex picture of reality. It would be foolish to generalize on the narrow base of one poem; but I can at any rate appeal to readers of Horace when I say that, though outstanding, this is not an unusual instance of this poet's art.

Now as long as you read this ancient satire like any modern poem (as we have done so far) you can be in no doubt as to its virtues. They lie in its personal character, its variable tone and matter, and the multiplicity of its patterns in spite of an unmistakable unity. In that sense it is poetry of a high order. But then, you have been reading it with modern spectacles, as though Horace has been writing for us. In historical perspective – poetry in Latin written by a Roman for Roman readers – it looks a different thing. How different does it look? Clearly, there are certain differences. The most important of them is this. According to the poet himself – and his contemporaries would have agreed with him – these poems, which we call satires, and the manuscripts, with a Horatian term, *sermones*, 'talks' – these poems are not really poetry. To him the genre is *satura* or *saturae* and *musa pedestris*, 'pedestrian verse'. So he says in the very poem we have been considering: 'what should I rather celebrate in the prose poetry of satire?', *quid prius illustrem saturis musaque pedestri?*[41] Here are echoes still of that earlier satire that grudged the name of poet to anyone writing as Horace does hinself, things that are closer to talk (or prose), *neque si qui scribat uti nos/sermoni propiora, putes hunc esse poetam.*[42] So some had said of comedy. Its metre apart, it is mere prose, *nisi quod pede certo/differt sermoni, sermo merus.*[43] What makes poetry is the eagerness of spirit and the force informing subject and diction.[44] Regularize rhythm and word order of satire, and you are left with prose; treat true poetry in the same manner, and you are left with the limbs of a poet, even though dismembered, *etiam disiecti membra poetae.*[45]

There are other indications of the same kind. Hence some critics have convinced themselves that Horace was not really much of a poet when he wrote satire. That assessment has a blunt edge. It leaves unexplained what it is meant to explain – the kind of poetry the satires are. It leaves unexplained too what Horace can possibly have in mind when he criticizes Lucilius, the archaic satirist, for his faulty workmanship;[46] when he makes astringent poetic demands for the writing of the New Satire;[47] and when all his life he publishes *sermones* that are worked to those demands.

How can this misunderstanding arise? What I think has happened is this. In retreating to Roman thought about Roman poetry we are retreating to a different intellectual climate, a climate of fixities, genres, and predetermined forms. When Horace is both apologetic and demanding about the poetic quality of his satires he is (in a sense) contradicting himself. He uses a language – the language of Graeco-Roman literary criticism – which had been developed to explain a different kind of poetry. The ancients had no critical vocabulary for describing verse that breaks through the limits of poetic forms thought to be fixed by nature. A poetic entity at varying levels of intensity and tone and not enshrined in the conventions of epic, drama, and lyric, is beyond their critical purview. Hence both of Horace's contentions are true, up to a point: satire is not poetry (like epic, drama, and lyric); yet satire demands the most astringent poetic workmanship if its blend of seriousness and gaiety is to succeed, and if the variety that ranges from poetic force to that of urbane humour and understatement is not to fall to pieces. Here is a large source of misunderstanding for the modern mind which is used to artistic representation without fixed and pre-established forms and genres. But the misunderstanding goes deeper. Scholars take Horace's ironies just literally enough to spring to his defence although they know all about ancient literary genres and although no one will charge them with lack of sensitivity to Roman poetry, or this poet's humour. Thus according to Professor Fraenkel, whose book has set a new scholarly standard in these studies, Horace remains a poet 'even in his *sermo pedester*' or he likes to disguise the change from one section of a *sermo* to another 'because there are not, or ought not to be, any sections in the talk of educated men of good manners.'[48] No, Horace's 'pedestrian Muse' is a form of poetry, as Professor Fraenkel himself has demonstrated so often and so well; and the poet disguises certain breaks between sections because a Horatian *sermo* stems from a unity of conception, and is not just adroitly fitted together of sections imitating the talk of educated men of good manners.

I will mention just one instance of this device. Expressing his gratitude for the farm in the first fifteen verses, the poet talks as if he were a countryman in the country, praising rural seclusion. Now, he adds, neither *ambitio* worries him, nor the climate of the city. But, as the reader realizes with a shock, what in fact follows is not praise of the country at all but dispraise of Rome. Thus the word 'city' is the turning point, and may be claimed as a 'concealed transition' from one 'section' to another. Yet it would be facile to regard these as two diverse paragraphs, riveted together by a third which may belong to either. Paragraphing is a useful reading aid in Horace. But these divisions are not the logical stages of conceptual prose, more or less strongly emphasized. The overall unity of this poem consists in a humorous balance of satisfaction and dissatisfaction, of country and town – a picture, I suggested, of human motivation. That unity is first hinted at in our passage, which links country and town, but cannot be fully perceived until its counterpart, a reverse transition from town to country, provides the indispensable clue.[49]

Listening to the claims and deprecations that Horace makes when he talks about his satires, what is our reaction? Satire is humorous. It is concerned with truth and morality. It has a multiplicity of style and tone – yes, all this may be agreed. It is not poetry – that surely is implausible. All Horace does in fact is to express the unusual variability of these poems in the nomenclature of his time, however ironically. Only by a strenuous intellectual effort can we enter into that way of thinking and the effort is well worth making. But I doubt if the teaching, unlike the manner, of Horace's literary criticism is the best way of understanding Horace the poet. At best these pronouncements help us to understand some of his preconceptions.

All his *sermones* have passages in what might be named a 'middle' or 'ordinary style,' itself a fusion of poetic and conversational elements. It is very flexible and casual. By a slight rise it can reach considerable intensity and seriousness. By a slight fall it easily reaches conversation, moral argument, and story-telling. Horace had predecessors using this poetic genre between genres. But no one before him seems to have grappled with the problem of how to make *sermo* the vehicle of serious poetry and how to infuse unity into this seemingly diverse world. That was a creative problem of the first order. In his best *sermones* – whether satire or epistle – he solved it in a manner which combined a maximum of diversity with a maximum of unity. This is the mainspring of his art and no imitation so long as the Horatian tradition persisted in European literature has ever achieved it again. All we can do is to sense it and describe it.

The *Hoc erat* is one of the finest examples of this manner and I have tried to describe it in two different ways. First we have read it as one might read a modern poem, not trying to make the historical adjustment to which classical scholars are accustomed. This I believe has certain advantages: the poem is allowed to speak without the distortions to which, as we have seen, ancient theory would subject it. Yet in projecting the *Hoc erat* to the contemporary screen we have distorted it in our own way. The only remedy for that is to do what we did in the second place, see it historically and remember why Horace and his contemporaries were dubious as to the poetic stature of a satire or poetic epistle. The two procedures are complementary. To treat them so, will help those of us concerned with the ancient literatures, and those concerned with the modern, to question our assumptions as well as theirs.

1. *Serm.* 2.6.1-3.
2. *Ibid.* 1 and 3.
3. *Ibid.* 3-4.
4. *Ibid.* 5.
5. *Ibid.* 14-15. Virg. *Ecl.* 6.4-5, said *pastorem, Tityre, pinguis/ pascere oportet ouis, deductum dicere carmen*. He adapted a Callimachean conceit, *Aetia*, 1, fr. 1.23-4 (cf. R. Pfeiffer's note). Horace seems to have given a further twist to the Virgilian passage although, doubtless, he remembered Callimachus as well.
6. *Serm.* 2.6.4.
7. 16-19.
8. 20.
9. 23-4.
10. 26.

11. 30-1.
12. 32.
13. 33.
14. 40-58.
15. 59.
16. 60.
17. 65.
18. 60-70.
19. 70-3.
20. 73-6.
21. 79-117
22. 77-8.
23. 78-9.
24. 73-4.
25. 30-1.
26. 32.
27. P. Lejay, *Oeuvres d'Horace, Satires*, p. 521, says, 'L'amour d'Horace pour la nature est un goût du citadin: la tranquillité, le silence, la liberté, surtout, sont les biens,' etc.
28. *Epodes*, 2.1.
29. *Epist*. 1.14.13.
30. *Serm*. 2.7.28-9; nor does Horace's liking for simple country fare escape scrutiny in the following verses.
31. *Carm*. 2.18.11-14.
32. *Serm*. 2.6.23-4.
33. 29; *quam rem* Bentley for *quas res MSS*.
34. 38-9.
35. 63.
36. 64.
37. 115-16.
38. 3-5.
39. Letter to John Wilson ('Christopher North'), *The Early Letters of William and Dorothy Wordsworth*, ed. E. de Selincourt, 1935, p. 295.
40. *Serm*. 2.6.77-8.
41. 17.
42. *Serm*. 1.4.41-2.
43. *Ibid*. 47-8.
44. 46-7.
45. 62.
46. *Serm*. 1.4 and 10.

47. *Serm.* 1.10.5ff., 40ff., 72ff.
48. E. Fraenkel, *Horace*, pp. 143, 393.
49. *Serm.* 2.6.59ff.

The Character of the Romans in their History and their Literature

FRANK ADCOCK

When I received the honorific invitation to deliver this lecture in memory of Professor Todd, I sought, as my predecessors have done, a topic that would reflect his interests and invoke the memory of his personality. This lecture is about the character of the Romans (– and Professor Todd's character was cast in a Roman mould –), but it is not limited to a psychological investigation into the ingredients of character, good or bad, which the Romans praised or blamed in themselves or in their fellow countrymen.

The list of these qualities would be long – from the *pietas* which Aeneas exhibits almost to excess,[1] as an old gentleman displays a white chrysanthemum at a wedding, to that quality of intolerant and intolerable arrogance for which the malice of Cicero coined the name '*Appietas*'[2] as he viewed his predecessor in the province of Cilicia, Appius Claudius Pulcher. The character of the Romans was always composite, and it reflects their history, if at times with that degree of refraction which justifies the ways of men to men. The ups and downs of their fortunes, their dangers and their triumphs; the impact of other peoples as they became their neighbours, their friends, their enemies or their subjects changed them, even if not so much as they changed some peoples of softer metal. And it is to be remembered that, from their very beginning, the Romans, that is, those who looked to the Seven Hills from whence came their help, were a composite people. For Rome, situated like Cambridge or Oxford at a river crossing, attracted to itself at once Latins and Sabines.[3] As a people they were like a homespun tweed in which differing strands were interwoven to form a tough material of a sort of colour easier to recognize than to define and describe. The island that makes a crossing of the swift-flowing Tiber easy marked its position[4] and was the geographical pivot of its history. The northern element, the Sabines, brought in a strong moral fibre which is praised from the elder Cato[5] to Horace,[6] the more praised as it assumed the flattering *aura* of antiquity.[7]

The community took its name from the city of Rome and was 'the People of Rome' as the American state is 'the People of the United States,' or the Athenian state 'the Athenians.' For Rome was the head of the body politic in a sense in which London is not the head of the British state or even Paris the head of France. Wherever a Roman was, his affections, like his roads, all led to Rome. And when Constantine at last shifted the balance of the Empire to the East, and founded the city that was soon called after him, the name *he* gave to it was, most probably, New Rome.[8]

Rome did not, like some great cities such as the one in which we meet, look to the sea: it looked to the land. The sea, so mutable, so un-Roman in its changing moods, did not match the Roman mind, which was rooted in the soil. For the Romans, were, above all, a peasant people, a race of the soil whose territory was, to begin with, the *ager*

Romanus, conquered by the sword and in subjection to the plough. Virgil was at his most Roman when he wrote his *Georgics*, the epic of the ffarmer – '*quid faciat laetas segetes*'[9] and so on. That was always the prosaic present of Rome, as *arma virumque* – the opening words of the *Aeneid* – was its romantic mythological past. To Cicero, who in such matters was a good judge, the People of Rome was a community bound together by a practical association of joint interest and common right,[10] and its state was the *res publica*, the people's business, the people's interests, and that was that.[11]

As in his home and household the *paterfamilias* had as his first duty the management of its affairs for its own good and no other, so to the Romans the conscientious, unselfregarding care for the people's interest was the duty of the magistrates, summed up in the short and pregnant word *fides*.[12] There was a time when the Roman community had been ruled by an alien aristocracy of conquerors, the Etruscans, who bequeathed to it a stronger, more comprehensive concept of ruling power than was given to any other ancient people so far as can be seen – symbolized by the *fasces*,[13] that businesslike combination of rods and axes, the sign of the *imperium* in its plentitude of power. And, when the alien rulers were driven out, the Roman Republic endured, for limited periods and in collegiality, the rule of the consuls no less unfettered than that of the Kings. What its rulers ordained was a command and what the people ordained was a command too. When the Roman people said 'yes' it was a command, as also when it said 'no' it was a prohibition; but its choice was limited by the belief that only in a multitude of counsellors there is wisdom, so that the ruler should be advised by the elder statesmen of the Senate and the people should only speak when it was spoken to. The citizen of Rome had the right, not to do what he would but to do no more than the laws enjoined on him, to suffer no more than the laws allowed. This to the Romans was 'liberty'[14] – a concept narrower and less intellecutal than the Greek *eleutheria*, and it was dangerous to encroach upon their liberty except, if need be, under the harsh constraint of war and in the field of war. For sufficient reason Romans were obedient, but only for sufficient reason enshrined in tradition which was the capitalized experience of statecraft as the skill of the farmer is the capitalized experience of his kind. The converse of this limit of liberty was the acceptance of the guidance of his betters, which was rewarded by their claim to be followed, obeyed and honoured. The legacy of aristocracy derived from the Etruscans endured to be the setting of the authority of the magistrate. A Roman demanded to be free: he did not demand to be equal, and if a Roman ever thought – in an imaginative moment – that men were born free and equal, he was apt to believe that equality was refuted by the facts of life once life began. There is no dictum more suited to a peasant than the dictum 'by their fruit you shall know them' and it was to the Roman self-evident that men who had ruled with wisdom and courage had proved their worth by that fact. And as the state prospered, the *mos maiorum* – the way things had been done – became the key to future success.

Thus the Romans were at once conservative and conventional, except that in war they were less allergic to innovation than most military nations have been.[15] This conservative character shortcircuited the need to think anew in most matters by the instinctive belief that experience which is gained from practice was the best guide where problems were recurrent, as they were to the Romans in the beginning of their advance to power; and this economy of thought was summed up in the idea of authority (*auctoritas*)[16] which assumed that power would be used conscientiously for the general good by those whose experience and inherited devotion to the community stood above question. And so far as the Romans revered their gods, their *pietas*, which they came to regard as a justification of their success, enjoined upon them the duty to play fair by the gods, if only because the gods, if negelected, could do more harm to the community than the community could do to the gods. Their religion was not a thing of emotion; it was honest dealing between men and heaven: precise, formal, conscientious, so that, if the farmer left his farm to go to war, the gods would do their best for the farm he left. Religion was, what it means, 'a bond' and a Roman's bond was indeed better than his word, or at least quite as good and more durable. The device of the hard-headed, hard-handed English king, Edward the First, was the two Latin words *pactum serva*, which was his brief answer to many problems even if it did not always apply. All these notions combined together to make the Romans as self-confident as they were self-centred.

But I must not dilate further upon the political institutions of the Romans. I have had my say about that elsewhere.[17] Most of the time, an ordinary Roman was not much concerned with such matters, provided his liberty was not encroached upon. When that happened they sought redress and protection by officers of their own, and the protection was granted to them. When we think away the political conflicts which later writers attributed to them in the manner of their own times, the main concern of the ordinary Roman in this stage with politics was really like that of the innkeeper in Dickens who was content, just now and then, 'to put on his boots and vote for the gentlemanly interest.' They remained, as I have said, rustic. They liked the country, its sounds and its smell, though the odour that most attracted them was the smell of a field that the Lord had blessed. They approved of the sea as a spectacle, storms and all, as Lucretius was to say.[18] They were fond of flowers and had an interesting vocabulary of colours. They did a little hunting in an amateurish way, and no doubt honest poachers laid their snares. But the nobles would rather ride than walk and rather be carried than ride. The Roman peasant rose early, worked hard, and lived an abstemious life. His betters, about whom there is more evidence available from the Middle Republic onwards, drank quite enough, ate too much and took too little excercise – except when campaigning. There is a passage in the *Natural History* of the Elder Eliny[19] which records the healthy effect on a Roman consul of a hard-fought battle on a hot day in the south of France.

Within their houses the *paterfamilias* ruled with a fine absolutism. For their womenfolk the Romans always had a high regard, being indeed more domesticated than the Greeks. Perhaps the most famous domestic interior in English poetry –

> For them no more the blazing hearth shall burn
> Or busy housewife ply her evening care:
> No children run to lisp their sire's return
> Or climb his knees the envied kiss to share.[20]

comes from a Roman poet,[21] save that he said it in two lines instead of Thomas Gray's four. In the highly intermarried and, if I may say so, inter-divorced best set of the late Republic, women had much influence not always ill-applied. But in *all* classes the Roman matron had more freedom, more responsibility, better treatment than has normally prevailed in the Mediterranean world. She enjoyed, in fact, the rare felicity of having what she wanted – though not rights. In general, the Romans of the early and middle Republic were rather dour: rather glum, though with some imagination at short range; hard bargainers, though fair-minded: singularly courageous in adversity, prudential and sagacious.

Such were the Romans, as such people in such a setting are apt to be. They were not prone to speculation; observant about what directly concerned them, as you may tell from Cato's work on Farming, but incurious about most things else. When a Roman wanted to say just what he meant – as he generally did – his native Latin, though less subtle than Greek, enabled him to say it with exactness and without ambiguity. And though, with time, Latin became more flexible, more metaphorical, inclined to repetition and a trifle pompous, it never lost, to judge from what remains of Latin in the Middle Republic, a sturdy quality, a robust emphasis that well expresses the people that created it. And when Latin became elegant what it meant by *elegance* was above all the right word in the right place.[22] The Roman aristocracy found its most intellectual activity in the formulation of law, but the quintessence of their statecraft is in the most Roman of all Roman maxims – the people's safety is the highest law – '*salus populi suprema lex*.' And so laboriously and slowly Rome grew to power – '*tantae molis erat Romanam condere gentem*.'[23] And with a sensible, unjealous liberality of mind – admired by people who did not practise it – they admitted to their citizenship some of their neighbours and, by and large, dealt fairly with the rest. Another instinct, their common sense, their toughness of spirit, had its reward. When Rome's interests conflicted with those of her neighbour, Rome caused her interests to prevail, if need be by war.

And Roman statecraft was shrewd in contriving that Rome made war with the odds on her side. War to the early Romans was not an adventure, a thing to be proud of, it was 'the continuation of policy by other means.' We think of the Romans as warlike, but no Roman writer glorified war. The Romans thought that peace was better than war; but that victory was better than defeat. One victory they nearly always made sure of, and that was victory in the final battle. And in success they were as wisely moderate as they were unyieldingly determined in adversity. Slowly Roman power extended, first over Central Italy, then over Southern Italy, then over the northern part of the peninsula. By skilful diplomacy the Romans turned old enemies into allies, from whom they asked nothing except that their military strength should be at the call of the Republic. By now, after the Republic had been going nearly three centuries, the Romans had formed a habit that was to be of great importance for the history of the ancient world. They limited their interference in the affairs of their neighbours to the minimum required by Roman security now and in the future. They prized what we would call the Roman way of life; they would die rather than surrender it; but they did not seek to impose it on others. Their restraint was rewarded by trust; and when the greatest enemy of Rome, Hannibal, invaded Italy and won resounding victories, the strong political system Rome had built up did not break down. Neither the Romans nor most of the Italians despaired of the Republic; and the solid strength of Rome triumphed over genius.

So far it is, you see, the somewhat prosaic story of a somewhat prosaic people, a people with shrewd instincts rather than bright ideas. For what we now call ideologies the Romans had little use. A Roman would not know what you meant if you spoke of an ideology, unless he was educated enough to be aware that it was bad Greek for an unroman thing. For, in good Greek ideology did not mean the pursuit of ethical or political ideas – it meant the study of physics.

And then, almost in her own despite, Rome ceased to be a purely Italian power and became a world power.

There were in the Mediterranean world at that time three great monarchies, which shared the inheritance of the Empire of Alexander the Great, two of them active, Macedon and Syria, one passive – Egypt. The first two crossed the path of Rome, and Rome broke them. Many smaller powers, willingly or unwillingly, became Roman satellites. And various areas passed under direct Roman control as provinces. Manpower, sagacity, courage, an instinctive judgment in war and diplomacy, together with a large admixture of good luck, had by the middle of the Second century BC made Rome dominant in the Mediterranean world. How did the homespun virtues of the Roman governing class wear in this new climate? I am afraid, they did not wear well. In their own circle, and under the eye of their equals, Roman nobles kept the old tradition of conscientiousness. But when Roman grandees went abroad to see that Rome got her way and her revenues, they were apt to leave consciences at home. They felt they could do pretty much what they liked, and the Senate, now the effective government in Rome, did not – perhaps could not – do enough to stop them. And the reasonableness of Roman policy was now punctuated by moments of impatient terrorism or phases of almost irrational malignity.[24] The philhellenism which made Rome admire the past of Greece did not always extend to its present. The Senatorial aristocracy was, by law or custom, debarred from trade and from making money at home, except through the ownership of land. It had become extravagant and spent more than its land would yield, so it was apt to make money by the spoils of war or the abuse of government abroad. The Roman nobility, now a closed circle of families that monopolized high office, was able and experienced, but class-conscious and conservative. It had, it is true, acquired a good deal of Greek culture and some understanding of Greek ideas. An eminent Greek philosopher, Panaetius, adapted the philosophy of Stoicism to make the best of the ethical ideas, the public spirit, the conscience of the Roman gentry. He produced a kind of philosophy of empire, which did proclaim Rome's duty to her subjects. Herein it was an appeal to what was best in the Roman governing class. But even enlightened Romans were so far pessimists that they looked back and not forward to find better days, or doubted whether more could be done than keep things as they were. Their statecraft was weak in the field of economics, for they only understood the economics of landowning, and they saw these only from above, from the angle of substantial landowners, which indeed they were. The idea of 'dignity,' of which I spoke earlier, became a danger. There were too many men who claimed it: the political stage became too crowded with actors, all burning to play the leading roles which they thought their due. The rule of the Senate was really a convention: the constitution still provided for the sovereignty of the People, when it was invoked. And well-intentioned men and, still more, ambitious men who could not get their way by working with the Senate, worked against it through the Assemblies of the People. But, with very few exceptions, all Roman political leaders were aristocrats, trying to defend or trying to win, their own way, their own advancement, their own dignity. Those who have often been called the democrats were not in the least concerned to secure that 'government of the People by the People and for the People should not perish from the earth.' They were not like men breasting the dawn up the hills of progress; they were like men trying to get on a bus, already overfull. Their intention was to drive it themselves, or at least collect the fares. And they are not made democrats by the fact that most of those already in the bus believed it to be, not a bus, but a tram.

And there were not in Rome what *we* know as parties, i.e., large political groups governed by principles and programmes to which they might not be unfaithful. For some eighty years after the nearest thing the Romans knew to democrats, the Gracchi,[25] had challenged the conventions of the constitution, and had perished, wars and civil wars, for short periods, thinned the political stage, but it filled up again – not, it is true, with the pantomime figures of depravity to which the conventional abuse of Roman political controversy reduced the good and bad alike. There were men of great capacity who sought good government, though hardly ever without an admixture of self-seeking. The Roman military machine became more and more efficient – the power of the Republic was extended to the Euphrates and the Rhine – but the legions were prone to serve their generals rather than the State. The competence and the ambition of the Roman aristocracy – for it was as competent as it was ambitious – reached its climax in Julius Caesar. With the impatience of a man who believed – not without reason – that no one else could do the job, he imposed a personal autocracy on the Roman Republic. The reaction of the older order – with its ideals and its illusions – was his assassination by men he had pardoned, men he had promoted, men for whom he cared. The ancient tradition, and Shakespeare, provided him with various last words, but there is a deep irony in the best attested of them all, in the indignant surprised cry that broke from the lips of the master of thirty legions 'Why this is violence.'[26] It was more than the dying words of a dictator – it was the epitaph of an age. The civil war that had made Caesar autocrat was followed by a civil war that avenged his death. And this was followed by a clash between his adopted son Octavian and his lieutenant Mark Antony. Antony of whom my friend Mr. Charlesworth once said that he was 'a great leader of men and a great follower of women.' became the consort of the last of the great Macedonian princesses, Cleopatra, who wished to revive the ancient power of Egypt. Octavian, cool, crafty and determined, became the leader, the Führer, of the Republican west, that had not endured an autocrat and would not endure the consort of a Hellenistic Queen. In seeking to move the centre of gravity of the Mediterranean world to the East, Antony, by his defeat, fixed it firmly in the West. The Roman world was reunited, and the day of an Eastern and Western Empire was postponed for centuries. Weakened by the blood-letting of three civil wars, the Roman aristocracy accepted the tactful rule of Octavian as the price of peace. And the Roman People rejoiced that the nightmare of civil wars was over. Octavian received the name of Augustus, and provides a most striking instance of the old poacher turned gamekeeper.

Meanwhile in the period of the Civil Wars, the effects of various social changes had worked themselves out. The wealth of Rome had drawn to the city an expensive *demi monde* often highly cultivated and accomplished, and Roman matrons undauntedly fought their rivals with their own weapons, good or bad.[27] The Second Estate, the Knights, are less visible to the political historian than the high aristocracy. Most of them were immersed in finance – their trade their politics – rallying to defend the State, and that – to them – meant defending the rights of property, the prestige of wealth and the security of overseas investments. Among the Knights there were doubtless many quiet, prudential, buttoned-up, cultivated gentlemen, like Cicero's friend, Atticus, but they did not set the vogue.

The Roman People were often indifferent, sometimes excitable, capable of generous enthusiasm and national pride. It has been said it is impossible to fool all the people all the time. Some Roman politicians, to do them justice, never ceased to attempt the impossible. There were, no doubt, at Rome and still more in the towns and villages of Italy, now included in the Roman state, many admirable thrifty orderly peasants, small shopkeepers and artisans. But little was done for them, and, in Rome itself, the riffraff riffed and raffed all over the place.

Augustus was not a man of genius in the sense that Alexander the Great or Napoleon deserve the name.[28] Nor was he a great Roman aristocrat like his adoptive father Caesar. He was sprung of the small Italian gentry with their hardheaded bourgeois virtues. And he substituted for the Republic of the aristocracy the Empire of the upper middle class. An astute manager of men, able to use those gifts in others which he did not himself possess, a laborious and clearsighted administrator, he reformed the government of the Roman provinces to their great advantage. He made the army his servant, and established a mechanism of government in which there were great careers for the great, and small careers for the small, but both under his own control. With the help of Agrippa, one of the greatest soldiers Rome ever produced, he advanced and strengthened the frontiers of the Empire, till it became a kernel of peace in a husk of war. Within the frontiers there was peace, a more enduring peace than the world had known before, or has known since. At a turning point in history he was one of the greatest servants of the human race.

Now I must look back and say something about the Romans as revealed by their literature, for the art of the early Republic, so far as it does not follow Greek models, is notable only for a strong veracity in portraiture.[29] Roman poetry had been slow to develop. Now and then, in the third and second centuries BC it had added to Greek forms memorable lines that had the peculiar weight and force that Latin could command; in comedy Plautus and

Terence borrowed from the Greeks, the one with native gusto, the other with a kind of grace. The elder Cato, who seems to have been of the intellecutal stamp of the scholar we are commemorating, brought a trenchant austerity of mind to the expression of sagacious common sense and thereby became a landmark in Roman literature and oratory. In the age of Caesar Catullus wrote lyrics that throb and burn with passion. He came from the Celtic North of Italy, from Verona. More truly Roman was Lucretius with his great didatic poem on the nature of the Universe. He was, if I may adapt a famous formula of A. E. Housman, a greater poet than Lord Rutherford, a greater physicist than Lord Byron; he vehemently urged, with missionary zeal, a Greek doctrine of release based on a Greek doctrine of an atomist universe with an atom that could not be split in a universe that could not be expanded. But he did it with a Roman directness and a Roman force. He was a man of nobility of spirit and eminence of mind, of notable dialectical vigour, and when he took time off to be just a poet, he was one of the greatest. I am not competent to assess him as a man of science – what even I can say is that no man of science can have had the root of the matter more deeply in him. Among historians there was Sallust, who assumed the mantle, but lacked the mind, of Thucydides. He was a good performer in his chosen style, who deserved the vogue he enjoyed under the Empire. He was a moralist for external application only, and one has to remember that truth is not the monopoly of the sincere. A more respectable historian was Asinius Pollio. A few phrases of his survive, which show him a man of impatient integrity with an astringent style. Caesar himself was an eminent orator and a writer who deserves more attention as a stylist than ingenuous youth has been able to give to him. And there was Varro, a man of immense and varied learning; a soldier of a kind; as Gibbon was a soldier of a kind when he was a captain in the Hampshire Grenadiers. Finally, there was Cicero, the man of this age whom we know best, a wit, an orator, an essayist, a letter writer, half a philosopher, more than half a statesman, a quarter of a poet, the most cultivated and civilized Roman of his day. A Polish scholar has said of him that his real biography began on the day of his death. For he had counted more than any other man in the spread and permanence of the fused culture of Greece and Rome, on which all European culture has drawn.

The new era of hope inaugurated by Augustus was the age of the greatest Roman poet Virgil, and the neatest, the most friendly, Roman poet Horace. I would admit that Virgil is inferior to Homer, but he is no more inferior to Homer than he is superior to Milton. And I admire Milton more than some modern critics. Of Horace I would only say that he only ceases to be a poet to those who believe that poetry begins where intelligibility ends. The long story of Rome was brilliantly described in a kind of prose epic by Livy, an honest man of letters and a master of narrative. But as, decade after decade, the reign of Augustus wore on, the pulse that had beat so high flagged. The welcome for what was new and the sense of high endeavour were dulled and in the field of philosophic speculation, of science, of mathematics, the Empire rested on its oars. There was learning and scholarship, but not the resolute adventurous pursuit of truth.

In Economics, the peace, the safety of the long roads and the paths of the sea, the fact that the Mediterranean world was securely one, meant a wide spread of industry and of the interchange of goods.[30] It was an era of multilateral trade. There was slavery, but good times made good masters, and the efficient – though perhaps too small – Roman army made but slight demands on the manpower of the Empire. In the century that followed the accession of Augustus the trade policy of the State was to leave well alone. Taxation was moderate and fairly distributed, and there was little exploitation of the provinces. In the Eastern half of the Empire the political and cultural liberalism of Rome permitted, and even encouraged, the permanence of Greek institutions and Greek art and letters, of which the Romans were unjealous connoisseurs. In the West, the Romans spread widely and took with them their language, their literature, and a form of municipal government that had taken shape within Italy. Of all the achievements of the Empire the romanization of the West was the most fruitful and the most enduring.

There were a few frontier wars, a few short-lived insurrections, a year of struggle for the throne when the dynasty that Augustus started had, at last, outstayed its welcome. But these troubles did not cut deep, and the next Emperor, Vespasian, who survived in the competition, was shrewd, hardheaded and competent. The Imperial machine ran by its own momentum, and to derail it meant chaos. The position of the Emperor, whose single will outweighed all other wills, was nearly that of an autocrat. But a near-autocrat was better than civil war. Even so, it was hard to reconcile with liberty in the ordinary sense. And if the State was the people's business as well as the public interest, the people had no say in their own business. Rome had, in fact, outgrown the political ideas of the Republic. And Vespasian's second son, Domitian, made this only too clear. The Roman upper classes were no longer his allies: for he had made them his enemies. They were reduced to insincere servility or silent hatred. On his death, the Roman aristocracy found its revenge in the account of the emperors written by Tacitus, the next great figure in Roman literature. He added to a respectable industry in the eliciting of facts, a diabolical insight into the upper layers of the human mind. Omelettes, I am assured, are not made without breaking eggs, and epigrams are not made without breaking truths. Tacitus was the most eminent maker of epigrams of all men who have written history. Compared with him, Gibbon is a maiden aunt. Latin has for many centuries been regarded as the right language for epitaphs written by a friend; Tacitus showed what it could achieve in the hands of an enemy. But, beyond that, he had a power of moving description, a quality of intellectual or emotional force, of effective composition that shows what history can claim to be as a literary art.

To return. A rather one-sided reconciliation between the Empire and liberty was found. It was found in the doctrine that the Emperor should be *the best man*, chosen to bear the heavy burden of being Emperor, and counting himself a servant as well as a master.[31] And the best man might be sought wherever he was to be found. The fact, or the assumption, that the Emperor was chosen out as *the best man* made the best people able to endure his rule without loss of self-respect. There follows a series of Emperors of provincial extraction who justified their choice. It is the reigns of these emperors which Gibbon, in a famous phrase, described as "the period of the world during which the condition of the human race was most happy and prosperous." And it was this in the Indian summer of the traditional civilization of the Ancient World.

As there had been a fusion of civilizations in literature, so during the period I have been describing there was a fusion of Greek artistic ideas with Roman.

To return once more to Augustus: the reliefs that are to be seen on the famous and beautiful Altar of Peace at Rome are not either of the old Roman type nor simply an imitation of Greek. There appears a composed dignity, a harmony of Greek and Roman ideas, and this governs the art of the Empire. Architecture shows the same kind of thing, reinforced by the Roman genius for engineering construction. There comes in a notable skill in making high buildings and great halls, especially by the use of true concrete, a characteristic Roman invention. In the western provinces art and architecture derive from Rome and are Imperial. It is the art and architecture, not so much of peoples as of an Empire, just as was Persian art in the days of the old Persian Empire. The great fire of Rome under Nero gave elbow room for architects; and painting, an art for which the Romans had a special aptitude, flourished, as can be seen at Pompeii till its destruction. Architecture became more complex and resourceful. The Roman armies, for instance, built very fine permanent installations. The narrative decoration, which suited the practical Roman mind appears on the Arch of Titus and the Column of Trajan, which are masterpieces in this manner. The general prosperity enriched men throughout the whole Empire, who were liberal in presenting their cities with handsome public buildings which may still be seen, most of all in Syria and North Africa. Gradually there are signs of separate provincial arts[32] and at Trèves there was an outcrop of something like baroque. And the truly Roman element in art is slowly submerged.

In education, which after all forms character, the Romans of the Empire assimilated their practice to that of the Greeks, and, as in some Greek cities, it became the concern of the State. The staple of education was rhetoric; this affected literature, partly because people practised declamation on a theme, partly because it became the fashion to write things to read aloud to one's friends. How long they remained your friends depended on what was read to them. The result of this fashion was that what the Romans now wrote had to have the arresting intelligibility of a modern broadcast. The Romans ceased to wish to see full-dress plays and preferred to see mimes. These might vary between something like the Grand Guignol, a ballet, or a single-handed performance like that of the late Miss Ruth Draper. The actors and actresses were often very skilful singers and dancers, highly paid, applauded – and despised. Apart from that, mimes were to the Romans rather what ordinary films are nowadays to ordinary people as contrasted with serious drama for serious people. Serious drama became something to be read in the study or the drawing room, not to be acted on the stage. There were novels and slight works of amusement, broader than they were long. In philosophy, Stocism was the fashion among the Roman upper class. Cynicism – which had not the character we call cynical – was, for the most part, a philosophy of the street corners preaching contempt for the allurements of the world. But Stoics or even Cynics might be either courtiers or martyrs or the private chaplains of the great. Science was comparatively sterile. In the *Questions about Nature* of Seneca you find an accumulation of observed phenomena, a kind of interest in the physical universe, but no real ardour to advance through experiment to speculation or to set back the borders of darkness. The great jurists of this and the succeeding age elevated the study of law to the philosophic justification of common sense and common humanity. Otherwise you have specialist works of a practical character but with a general background of knowledge: few books are more truly Roman than that of Vitruvius on Architecture, which is a triumph of mind over matter. But you may have your feet so firmly planted on the ground that you cannot advance, and there is in general a flatfooted quality about Roman intellectualism at this time.

You may have observed that at the beginning of this lecture I manoeuvred across from Rome to the Romans, and now it is time for me to manoeuvre back again. For by now the Romans are being absorbed as it were, into the Roman Empire. It is no longer the descendants of the pure-blooded Romans or even the Roman-Italian race that bear the burden, that fill the legions and monopolize the central administration. First the romanized West and then the hellenized East take a share in the central government. In the reign of the emperor Hadrian the Senate contained only one member of the ancient patrician aristocracy of Rome. There he was, preserved like a fly in amber to show it was the genuine article. But the tradition of Roman statecraft governed the State. Marcus Aurelius wrote his famous *Meditations* in Greek, not in Latin, but he did so in the time he could spare from arduous campaigning as one of the great soldier rulers of Rome in the Roman tradition. By this time, the impact of barbarian invasions was already dinting the rather too closely drawn frontiers of the Empire. When the predecessor of Marcus Aurelius was dying he gave as the watchword of the day 'Equanimity,' and it perished with him. The golden age of a prosperous world, based on the ancient civilization and ideals of Greece and Rome was passing away. The choice of the best man was replaced by the self-choice of ambitious soldiers, who ruled as undisguised autocrats. A prolonged period of wars, made worse by plagues and economic dislocation, threatened the prosperity, the unity, and the defences of the Empire. In the effort to survive, the old liberalism and freedom were replaced by a rigorous bureaucracy and a caste-system that stifled initiative and enterprise. And though slavery declined, a kind of serfdom grew. More and more the citizen was the slave of the State instead of the State the servant of the citizen. At last a series of soldier emperors from what is now Yugoslavia restored the territorial unity of the Empire and drove back the barbarian. These emperors were not Romans by birth, but they held firmly – in a sergeant major kind of way – to the old tradition of pagan Rome. It seemed to them that the Christian Church, now organized from end to end of the Empire, threatened its military and religious morale. But persecution closed the ranks of the Church, and it was too strong to yield. And then Constantine, by what was, at the lowest, a great act of statesmanship, reinforced the State by linking with it the Church.

This was destined to have a great effect on the course of civilization. For, in the Dark Ages, the Church shielded the flickering light of Roman culture and Roman intellectual disciplines. Through Saint Augustine and other Fathers of the Church classical philosophy was kept alive, converted to the service of Christianity and so, in this guise, transmitted to modern times. The Canon Law of the Church perserved the inheritance of Roman jurisprudence. Latin, the language of Churchmen, lived on to become the international language of the Middle Ages, not only for diplomacy and polite conversation or the impolite songs of wandering students, but for philosophical debate and scientific inquiry. This heritage continued, until Bacon and Milton, Newton and Copernicus, Descartes and Spinoza wrote some or all of their best work in Latin.

In the great shipwreck of the Western Emprie much of the civilization which Rome had fostered was to perish. But not all. There still stood on guard for a thousand years the Eastern Empire based on Constantinople, theocratic, formalized, almost ossified, but with an indomitable permanence. Roman Law – the greatest intellectual achievement of the Roman aristocracy – was preserved to be codified by Justinian. And Rome lived on in the romance languages of the west. The great roads, the splendid bridges and aqueducts, the buildings in which Roman architects revealed the wealth and public spirit of Italy and the provinces, remained. The arts of the government which the Republic and the Empire had devised for their own power and the ordering of the world in peace were not wholly lost. It had been Rome's practice to learn from her enemies: now her enemies learned from Rome, and what they learned, lasted. And so my story ends. It is no doubt true that other ancient peoples, above all the Greeks, surpassed the Romans in the illumination of the human mind and the liberation of the human spirit. But with the limits that their character has set to their activity, the Romans were the toughest, the strongest, the most enduring, and, on balance, the most beneficent of the peoples of the Ancient World.

1. E.g. Virg., *Aen.* 1.378.
2. Cic. *Fam.* 3.7.5.
3. See H. Last in *Camb. Anc. Hist.* VII, 493f.
4. Virg. *Aen.*, 8.85f. see H. Last, *ibid.*, 347.
5. *Orig.* fr. 51 Peter.
6. *Odes* 3.6.37ff.
7. Virg. *Georg.* 2.532.
8. See N. H. Baynes in *Camb. Anc. Hist.* XII, 697, n.1.
9. 1.1.ff.
10. *De Re Pub.* 1.39.
11. See H. Drexler in *MAIA* IV (1957) 247ff.
12. See E. Fraenkel 'Zur Geschichte des Wortes *fides*,' *Rhein. Mus.* 1916, 187ff.; R. Heinze, 'Fides,' *Hermes*, 1920, 140ff.
13. Last, *ibid.*, 384f.
14. See Ch. Wirszubski, *Libertas as a Political Idea at Rome, etc.* (Cambridge Univ. Press, 1950), 7ff.
15. See *Ineditum Vaticanum*, text published in Hermes 1892, 118ff.
16. R. Heinze, 'Auctoritas,' *Hermes* 1925, 384ff.
17. See *Roman Political Ideas and Practice* (Univ. of Michigan Press, 1959.)
18. *De Rer. Nat.* 2.1-2.
19. 7.50.166.
20. T. Gray, *Elegy written in a Country Churchyard*, lines 21-24.
21. Lucr. *De Rer. Nat.* 3.894-6.

22. E. E. Sikes in *Camb. Anc. Hist.* IX, 764.

23. Virg. *Aen.* 1.33.

24. See 'Delenda est Carthago,' *Camb. Hist. Journal*, 1946, 127f.

25. See Last, in *Camb. Anc. Hist.* IX 89ff.

26. 'Ista quidem uis est.' Suet. *Div. Iul.* 82.

27. See, for example, the description of Sempronia in Sallust *Catil.*, 25.

28. See *Camb. Anc. Hist.* X, 596.

29. See E. Strong in *Camb. Anc. Hist.* IX, 811ff.

30. See F. Oertel in *Camb. Anc. Hist.* X, 412ff.

31. Pliny, *Paneg.* 7.6. See F. E. Adcock, *Roman Political Ideas and Practice*, 95f.

32. See G. Rodenwaldt in *Camb. Anc. Hist.* XI, 803ff.

The Initiation of Aeneas

JOHN SHEPPARD

When I heard I was to have the privilege of meeting you in Sydney, that City Beautiful of which so many gallant young Australians had told me, I wrote, of course, to tell my friend and teacher, Dr. Gilbert Murray, the inspired interpreter of what is best and kindest in the Classics, and I asked him, since I knew that he was born here but had left Australia as a boy, eleven years of age, whether he began his classics here or later. To my delight he answered that he learnt his first Greek at a school in the bush, at Mittagong, from a grandson or great-nephew of the poet Southey. How appropriate that Murray should have learnt his first Greek from the kinsman of a poet. 'In my first Greek lesson,' he wrote, 'I was reading Μοῦσα, and Southey puzzled me by calling it ἡ Μοῦσα, which made me for a moment think the μ must be an η, so that I called it ἡοῦσα and disgraced myself.' How delightful that the first of all his brilliant emendations gave a new name to the muse he loves so well.

To-day we join in honouring the memory of a devoted teacher and a lover of the classics, and especially of Latin

– Frederick Todd. I never met him, but have heard, as most of you have heard, of his deep interest in his pupils, his rare gift for graceful composition, and the pleasure which he used to give his friends by declaiming to them some of his best-loved passages from Virgil. Certainly Todd, the author of your *Campanarum Canticum*, was, in the true Virgilian sense, a *pius vates*, a dedicated teacher, one of those of whom the poet says 'They have made some remember them by being worth remembrance' –

sui memores aliquos fecere merendo.[1]

How many sacred memories that phrase suggests to all of us. Will you, before I speak of the Initation of Aeneas, share with me some that have been much in my thoughts during my visit to your country?

The first Australian who ever came to King's was a priest, *sacerdos castus*, Frederick Sharland. He came to us from Hobart High School in 1867, just two years after good king Henry's Cambridge family opened its gates to boys from other schools than Eton. Three years later he was ordained and returned to Hobart to begin a faithful ministry of half a century.

Two others, whom I specially remember, were scholars of my own first year at King's. One of them, Wilfred Agar, was an English boy and presently became a Fellow of the College. In later life, for twenty years, he was beloved and honoured as Professor of Zoology at Melbourne. The other was George Lewis Blake Concanon, who came to us from Brisbane. After only one year with us he went home, I know not why. What I do know is that at Gallipoli he gave his life *ob patriam*, and that his name is written on our War Memorial at King's.

Yet another boy who was at Hobart School when Sharland was a curate was to prove a man of genius, wonderfully gifted, wonderfully modest – Lyndhurst

Giblin. He surpassed Aeneas in his *pietas*, deep loyalty of spirit, but in many ways was much more like Odysseus, that great-hearted, much-enduring hero. Only he was not self-centred as Odysseus was. He gave himself for others. Certainly he was 'a man of many devices.' He could make his own clothes, bake his own bread, teach a little boy to make his own toys, help him to enjoy good books, and later, if he showed good promise, 'rub up' his own Greek and introduce the lad to Homer or the plays of Aeschylus. By turn a Cambridge Blue, a Senior Optime in Mathematics, a gold-digger, a muleteer, a lumberjack, a merchant seaman, what he loved best was his home on the Tasmanian farm from which, like Cincinnatus, he was called to serve the State, first in the war of 1914, then much later in what proved the most exacting and most fruitful service of his life, the unsolicited professorship at Melbourne, and those other grave responsibilites he bore so quietly, so nobly, and with such advantage to us all. We at Cambridge loved him too. It was a joy to us in 1937-8 that for some months he lived with us, as a Fellow of the College, and I know, in 1948, it was a joy to him to help us with advice in the creation of the studentship for young Australian graduates which bears his name.

Thinking of him and of those other memories, I ask you now to come with Virgil to a little port near Naples, Cumae, and to watch, through Virgil's eyes, the first arrival of the Trojan pilgrim fathers in their promised land of Italy. No sooner were the anchors down than 'in a flash' the young men were ashore – *juvenum manus emicat ardens*[2] – scouring the countryside. 'Plenty of water here!' 'What splendid timber!' 'Flints for firing!' Everything, in fact, they need for building their new Troy. Everything? Their leader, who knew better, went at once to pray and to seek guidance. He knew, man does not live by bread alone, but by the word. In the vestibule of Apollo's ancient temple he and his companions paused a while to gaze with wonder at a series of strange frescoes, symbols of a prehistoric Cretan mystery, a tale of hate and cruelty and of their nemesis, of grim perverted lust, but also of the pity which can sometimes turn the worst of what we suffer to a seed of something infinitely precious. First there was a picture of Androgeos, the Cretan envoy, treacherously killed by Athens, then of the Athenian youths and maidens sacrificed in barbarous requital. Here were depicted the grim secrets of the Labyrinth; there the pity of the master-craftsman Daedalus, his flight to Cumae, and his unfinished picture of the boy, his child, who did not heed his warning and who died because he flew too near the sun.

Have we not sometimes in our own dark days remembered Icarus, and said, 'It was the purest light of heaven for whose fair sake they fell'?

Examining these pictures, brooding on their meaning, they would have lingered still had not the Sibyl's voice abruptly called Aeneas –

> This is no time for poring over those works of art.
> Just now you would do best to sacrifice, seven bullocks
> That have not yet been yoked and as many properly
> chosen sheep.[3]

It is indeed a somewhat harsh and abrupt challenge. I have ventured to quote the version given us by Mr. Day Lewis, because it renders so faithfully the Sibyl's brusque and agitated intervention. It has been suggested by a great authority, the late Dr. Mackail, that Virgil, had he lived to make a last revision, would have rounded off her paragraph and made it smooth by adding something. I can't think so. To me the Sibyl's call seems greatly needed, and the fact that it is brisk, and barely courteous, makes it all the more effective. Do we not remember – certainly the Sibyl does – that in Carthage long ago Aeneas brooded on a set of pictures?[4] They were scenes of Troy, and at the sight of them Aeneas cried: 'Here, even here, honour is paid with honour and they weep because such things are true.' After all, he began to think, this people, with their wonderful new city, happily already building, are not savages; they pity what is pitiful, they honour what is good. It is the first step in the process which will end in tragedy for him and Dido. Longing as he does, and always will, for an end of his unhappy pilgrimage, he very soon begins to think that, after all, perhaps a settled home in Carthage might be a solution not rejected by the gods. Who knows? So he had felt in Crete not long ago, and would begin to feel again in Sicily. Perhaps, in spite of all . . . ?

So at Carthage he looked back, not forward, and almost, not quite, forgot his duty and his mission. Here at Cumae he has much to learn. He has to see a vision of the glory of the future and be strengthened by it. Better still, he has to learn, as he has never learnt before, the secret of the tragic paradox that makes life worth the living not in spite of its inevitable hardships, but because of them. If he is to become a worthy leader of his people and a worthy father of the Roman race, he has to understand that mystery – no, not quite understand it – no one can – but recognize it, feel it, learn from it, and even so be strengthened for his task.

I suggest to you that not the Sixth book only, but the whole Aeneid is the tale of the initiation – education, if you will – of a good man, but not, at first at any rate, a very great man, for a mission which entails a burden of responsibility so heavy that it well might seem to us beyond the powers of any man. For such a task he needs indeed the qualities of which we have already seen in him the promise, but not as yet the ripeness, the achievement. That is still to come. Again and yet again, not only in the Dido episode, which is a climax and a grave defeat – not irretrievable, but grave – some of us have felt, if not, with Charles James Fox, the man is 'odious' or 'insipid,' certainly that the wise and courteous words of Dryden are just a little kinder than our own uncharitable thoughts. 'On the whole matter, humanly speaking,' we all 'doubt there was a fault somewhere.' A fault in Aeneas? Yes, and in Dido too. But in the poet? I don't think so. I think he meant us to face facts and recognize that even heroes are not ready-made, impeccable, and that sometimes, for a very great mission, destiny, or Jupiter, or whatever power we reverence, does choose what seems a most imperfect human instrument. In the Prologue Virgil didn't say 'the glorious Aeneas,' as Homer said 'the glorious Achilles' and even 'the glorious Odysseus.' Why? Because his theme will not be 'glorious Aeneas,' but the way in which a loyal-hearted man with many failings learns to play his part with others in the service first of Rome herself and then of all the Roman race.

In the light of that intention, is it still astonishing – is it a sign of Virgil's failure? – that he introduces his Aeneas for the first time in a crisis in which many of us think – I don't say I do -- that we should behave at least a little better than the hero. A hurricane is coming. The sky lours, lightning flashes, the sea is turbulent and the winds clearly threaten shipwreck, yet Aeneas doesn't, as the Admiral of the whole fleet, vouchsafe his men a word of encouragement – 'Good cheer, my hearties' – he doesn't take the helm . . . he gives no orders . . . Simply he lifts his hands in horror, and shouts aloud how much he wishes he had died at Troy.[5] The fact is, he is nearly at the end of his tether. He is, for the moment, almost a nervous wreck. His quality is shown next morning, when he has recovered, and he does quite well for the rest of the day. But we are warned. We know now what the strain on him has been, and sympathize. We understand much better why, from time to time, he fails. There is a fault, he is a human creature, subject to our human weakness. So, I venture to say, was Charles James Fox, if he had only known it. Virgil has done what he intended, and has given us the clue. The man is deeply loyal to his duty, when he sees it plainly; he is kind and grieves for human sorrow; on occasion he can show fine leadership. But far too often he still lacks decision; his imagination is not disciplined; his human sympathy itself sometimes becomes a source of weakness; and, above all, he lacks, not faith exactly, but the zest for life which kindles hope and strengthens faith itself. His need is not to be 'converted' but to be 'fired' in spirit. That, you will find, is the poet's own word at the end of the great experience at Cumae. Anchises, having shown his son the vision of Rome's grandeur, and her spiritual mission, 'fires his soul' with a passionate love of his great future –

incenditque animum famae venientis amore.[6]

So much for the Sibyl's rough, but necessary call to action. It has taught us something. But here is another curious example of what scholars call 'a difficulty' or 'a crux.' The prophet Helenus, you may perhaps remember, in Book III,[7] informed Aeneas that the Sibyl, if he could persuade her not to trust her oracles to easily mislaid and scattered papers, nor to couch them, like some modern planners, in an unintelligible jargon, will provide him with particulars about the peoples he will have to meet in Italy, the wars he will have to fight, and generally how he is to cope with difficulties or evade them. All this she will 'map out' for him, the prophet says –

expediet cursumque dabit.

'Oh dear!' some learned scholars cry, 'Oh dear, she does

nothing of the kind!' Has Virgil blundered? Well, they say, not quite as bad as that. If he had lived to revise the whole work, he would probably have altered what the prophet said.[8]

I think not. In his first prayer to the Sibyl, Aeneas, so it seems to me, expects the sort of thing the prophet told him she would give him. Indeed, he almost dutifully asks for it, before he mentions a much greater boon, much nearer to his heart and much more difficult to ask with faith: 'I want to go down to the other world and see my Father.' 'War awaits you still,' she says, 'a Tiber for a Simois, a new Achilles,' and of course, in her own complicated and at times quiet unintelligible fashion, she might well have gone on to explain the details . . . but he cries 'All this I know. For all I am prepared. But first, my Father!'[9]

How ungrateful and how odd some of us are. That exclamation marks the moment when Aeneas does begin to look as if, with all his conscientious scruples, all his tendency to doubt and brood and blunder, and almost despair, he really is to be the sort of hero that Anchises and the rest of us, indeed the world and Jupiter himself, require if the new Troy is not to be a failure. This is the moment we have waited for so long, and just to mark that moment Virgil has made Aeneas dutifully listen while the Sibyl starts to give him just what Helenus suggested, her ethnological map of Italy and her handlist of campaigning tactics, but break in impatiently before she has the time to sort her papers and expand her periods, and tell her: 'What I really want is to see Father.' I for one love him for it, and I'm grateful to the prophet (if he knew about this grand adventure) for not telling him about it in advance. He left that theme alone – or, if you please, he very wisely left it to Anchises. That's a different matter, and, of course, Anchises, knowing what his son is like, has had many anxious moments, but believes the lad will come.

Anyhow, Aeneas does it, and some of us love him for it. By a curious coincidence – or is it merely a coincidence? – just the same sort of learned persons find a 'difficulty' in the *Odyssey* on precisely the same kind of point. When Circe, recognizing the great power of the herb Moly, acknowledges Odysseus as her master, and restores his crew to human shape, we might well think that the episode was at an end. But no! Their joy at the recovery and the miraculous union with their friends leads to a scene of such hysteria that Circe, by no magic arts but just a woman's way, enchants them all again.[10] 'Poor dears,' she says, 'you've had a terrible time in your adventures, and you've quite forgotten how to enjoy yourselves. Stay here and recover your tone.' So they stayed, and she gave them a good time (thanks to Moly, with no fear of consequences), till, after a whole year of it, the crew themselves – not Odysseus, mark you – thought it really must be time to go.

So Odysseus asked her most politely for permission and she graciously consented. 'Heaven forbid I should keep you, if you really will be grim. You'll have to visit the dim country of the dead in order to consult Teiresias. He'll plot your course for you and give you all directions.' In the sequel, to the consternation of what Mr. F. L. Lucas calls the 'owls' of scholarship, Teiresias does nothing of the kind. And why? Odysseus carries out the necessary ritual, keeps off the shades, except his own unlucky friend Elpenor, till Teiresias is ready; and the prophet gives him the most strict injunction not to eat or let his comrades eat the Sun-god's cattle, drops a hint or two about the situation he will find at home – the first hints that Odysseus has yet had of trouble there – but tells him nothing, not a word, about the rest of his homeward voyage. Why? Is it as some Germans gladly tell us, and some Englishmen resignedly repeat, that Homer here has blundered – or perhaps it isn't Homer at all? I can't agree. Consider what has happened. After the solemn warning about the Sun-god's cattle and the hints of trouble nearer home, Odysseus could so easily have asked him to continue iwth the promised plotting of his course, etc. He doesn't. Why? Unpractical, not like a fuehrer. The truth is that he wants to talo talk to Mother.[11] That, to some of us, is surely touching. I for one am very glad of it, because this is the first of many things in this brave story of the hero's visit to the shades – by sea, of course, because he is a sailor – which throw for us a new light on his character, a new light on Homer's spirit too, the same loving spirit which shapes both his tales, and makes him in his own most human way the prophet and forerunner and inspirer of the spirit which we call Virgilian and even Christian. His Odysseus doesn't so much want to have his course mapped out; he wants to talk to Mother. And, she tells him, she has no fresh news of home. All was much the same there, when she died, except that she was pining for his loving kindness and the light had gone out for her.

That, I assure you, is the work of the same poet who created an Achilles, in his right mind merciful to captives, a youth who hated a lie, and who dreamt of honour and the praise of men; then in the nemesis of his own pride and his great error, learnt that he cared far more for friendship than for glory –

> Mother, all these things indeed hath Zeus accomplishéd,
> But what profit is there in these things. My friend is dead . . .
> and I did not help him.[12]

And again, that same Achilles, when he vainly tries to make amends for his great fault by vengeance, has to learn that vengeance too is vanity compared with simple human feeling, so that he spares and honours Priam, though he fears himself, lest passion come again. Such a poet is not lightly disregarded when we study Virgil, Dante or the Gospels. He who made Achilles in his pity for Patroclus say 'You weep like a little girl who runs behind her mother, plucking at her skirts and begging to be taken in her arms'[13] was loved by him who made the little boy Iulus slip his hand into his father's hand and plod upon his way with him, *non passibus aequis*.

The initiation of Aeneas is, I venture to suggest, essentially initiation into thoughts like these.

The Golden Bough, found through the guidance of his mother's doves, will make it possible for him to go and to return unscathed, nay armed with something better than a map, a plan of operations, a spirit strong in hope, a heart made kinder, more intelligent by human pity,

> ibant obscuri sola sub nocte per umbram.[14]

I am reminded of some words which were quoted for our help in the dark days by our beloved King George VI: 'I said to the man who stood at the gate of the year, 'Give me a light that I may tread safely into the unknown.' And he replied: 'Go out into the darkness and put your hand into the hand of God. That shall be to you better than light and safer than a known way.' '

At the threshold of the shadow-world are symbols of our common lot, anxiety, disease, old age; fear, hunger, poverty and death; toil, and for solace, death's kind brother sleep; mischievous joys which hurt us in the long run: furies and discord, frenzied, poisonous. All these are facts which we must know, and sometimes must accept, if life is to be fruitful and our quest not vain.

But yonder, in the Elm of Superstition, are swarming creatures of our own imagination, monsters against which no weapon except reason and a clean imagination can avail. Life is hard, but need not be so hard as our own superstition makes it.

So we come to the grim ferryman and the souls, as numerous as fallen leaves in autumn and as birds that gather at the season of migration. All are eager to pass over to the other side –

> tendebantque manus ripae ulterioris amore.[15]

What did the poet mean? The same, I think, as he meant in the later, larger vision. Surely that life still beckons always, here and everywhere, and perhaps hereafter. The spirit moves us still, and we must needs press on, whatever may await us.

When we have passed the river and hear voices[16] on the further shore of infants wailing for the light of life they never knew, because they died at the mother's breast; of men condemned to death unjustly; of innocents whose poverty and grinding toil became so hateful to them that they threw their lives away, and women to whom love brought an untimely death, and warriors, cut off in battle, I confess that I am moved, and don't much care to question why each company is there. Virgil, the learned scholars tell us, either did not know Professor Norden's admirable theory or, if he knew it, didn't think it worth his notice. Very shocking! Dr. Norden's theory is that by an ancient superstition those who died untimely had to wander without rest until the term of their natural life was ended. But if Virgil really knew this, he has blundered about several details, and of course it is, so we are told, 'a positive blemish' that he does not give the necessary explanation of their presence here – it would only, after all, take a few lines. So my learned friends conclude, 'it is more respectful' to the poet's reputation to suppose that, had he lived, he would have rewritten the whole passage. Also, had he lived, he would have changed his reference to Minos, who, we are told, has no right to be here. That, say my friends, is the most 'charitable' assumption.[17]

But, seriously, who in the world except the learned critic wants an explanation? If we listen simply to the poet without too much ingenuity, we shall understand. Here are children who have died, we say, untimely. That is common. Virgil wishes his Aeneas, and his readers, to remember that. Men have been condemned to death unjustly. That also happens. So does suicide by very gentle, innocent people, and men and women have indeed been known to kill themselves or others, because of misdirected love or jealousy or that despair of love which really is not love at all. And some, we know too well, have died in war.

These things the poet chose to place at the beginning of the revelation to Aeneas of the meaning of all life – life here, as well as life hereafter and life not as it might be if desire came true but as it is, so long as we are what we are. These things are true, and Minos is a kinder judge than Rhadamanthus. That is a good reason for his presence. He will judge these spirits mercifully, and assign each to a lodging – but a lodging only on a pilgrimage, for them, as for us all.

Therefore, because he has just seen and felt these things, when Dido passes, cold, aloof and silent, and rejoins Sychaeus, the true love of all her life, Aeneas for the first time fully understands what he has done, confesses and breaks down in tears of pity, not for himself, but her.

Why did the poet make Aeneas meet Deiphobus just after that great moment? Deiphobus was horribly mutilated, on that last grim night of Troy, through Helen's treachery and cruelty. He had lived with her as a lover, but on that black night, unarmed and undefended, he slept while she brought Menelaus to the house and had her lover murdered by her husband. Why remind us of that hateful incident just now?

I think it was because on that same night at Troy Aeneas very nearly left his father and his wife and child quite undefended in the home while he was desperately seeking death in what he knew was futile, hopeless fighting. Hector's spirit had come to him and told him 'Troy is lost. Do not attempt to fight any more, but save the gods of Troy and carry them away abroad to safety.' But Aeneas, when he heard the noise of fighting in the streets, rushed out to fight again. It was a fault for which we cannot blame him, but it was a fault. And when at last he heard the Queen's sad cry, and saw the mutilated body of old Priam, suddenly he knew where duty lay.

> Then, then, for the first time fierce horror came on me. I stood appalled. I seemed to see my own dear father's form, my wife deserted, and my house in ruins, and the fate of my dear little son.[18]

Those lines were read by Shakespeare at the Stratford Grammar School, and to some purpose. That is why Hamlet let Polonius stop the player at the point, dismissed him courteously, and railed upon himself.

Aeneas rushed at last, at long last, to his duty, and at that moment suddenly met Helen, and his impulse was to kill her. But his mother's voice came to him and rebuked him. 'First your father and your wife and little son.'

Well, well, all that is now a memory. Aeneas by this time has learnt his lesson. Virgil has not recorded any comment from him on the story told him by Deiphobus. Indeed what could he say? Aeneas is no criminal, but a good man, sorely tried and much perplexed. There is no need for him to see the fate of souls whose guilt is past redemption. It is enough for him to hear the Sibyl's warning and to pass out from the realm of darkness to the light and the pure air of the Elysian plain. And there, what does he see?[19]

First athletes, still rejoicing in their games. How kind that intuition of our poet was. Then, at the centre of the picture, Orpheus with a choir of dancers and of singers, teaching them, we imagine, a new, better song; then, balancing the athletes, Knights of Troy, at peace, but still as proud as ever of their cars and weapons, still as kind as ever to their horses.

All these he passed, and entered a sequestered fragrant laurel-grove, where a serene, grave company were either feasting or just risen from their places for their grace after meal, Apollo's paean. Who were these?

Some who had suffered and were wounded, fighting to defend their fatherland; some priests whose lives were priestly; poets and teachers, faithful to their calling, whose words were worthy of Apollo, and others who by arts they had discovered made life civilized – that is a little gentler, better ordered. And last, not least, those who made some remember them by being worth it.

Not all are here who will be. Some are still on their way. Who knows? Perhaps, by Minos' leave, some of those children? Some unhappy lovers? Nor will all stay here for ever. Some, though happy here, press on to further trials, further service.

> Hic manus ob patriam pugnando volnera passi,
> Quique sacerdotes casti, dum vita manebat,
> Quique pii vates et Phoebo digna locuti,
> Inventas aut qui vitam excoluere per artis,
> Quique sui memores aliquos fecere merendo.[19]

Great as they are, these noble lines are still an introduction to an even nobler theme. Virgil is rising to the height of his great argument. Now we are ready for the meeting of the father with the son, the father's cry 'At last! My son, I knew that you would come. I knew your loyalty would conquer all the difficulties and the dangers of the way. I have been counting the days,' and for the revelation of the wonder of the world, the mystery of life and suffering and hope. 'Why', asks Aeneas, still depressed, still anxious, 'Why are these souls possessed by this insane desire to live again on earth?' The answer comes '*Spiritus intus alit* . . .' and finally he sees the pageant which reveals the hope, the glory and the grandeur which is Rome. After that Aeneas is to be a different man, at last a hero, worthy of the name and of his mission.

Until that time, as we have seen, although Aeneas has been learning, very slowly, and with many setbacks and backslidings, he has never satisfied us, never satisfied his modern critics. I think the poet meant us to feel like that. I think it was his purpose from the outset.

Think again of his prologue Arms and the man . . . fate's refugee . . . the wrath of Juno . . . the Penates . . . Latium . . . the Alban fathers and the walls of Rome. Juno's appalling persecution of the man, distinguished for his *pietas*, Juno's great scheme for Carthage . . . the founding of the Roman race. A greater theme than any man's achievements, a greater load than almost any man could bear.

Contrast that with the Prelude of the *Iliad*, . . . Achilles . . . Wrath . . . grief . . . death . . . the will of Zeus . . . the glorious Achilles. There is the whole plot of the *Iliad*, from the first calling by Achilles of the Greek assembly to the moment when he cries 'Mother, all these things indeed hath Zeus accomplished but what profit is there in these things; my friend is dead'; and again after the appalling sequel and the hero's loss almost of his humanity, to the word of Zeus, 'This is the honour that I give him,'[20] to be himself again, a man in his right senses, merciful.

Now let us look again at the multitude of souls that throng, like murmurous bees, to drink the waters of oblivion and be reborn. Aeneas asks – he has to ask it –

just as Scipio, in his dream of heavenly music, had to ask, 'Why should we not stay here? Why go back to the stress and strain of life?' So now Aeneas asks, 'Father, how can it be? Unhappy souls, why does this fearful craving for the life of earth possess them'?

Is it possibly for the same reason for which hands, so long ago, were stretched out for the love of the further shore? We have now reached the culminating moment of the vison. Let me read you part of Dryden's version, because Dryden better than the rest, I think, has understood the poet's thought.

> Know first that heaven, and earth's compacted frame,
> And flowing waters, and the starry flame,
> And both the radiant lights, one common soul
> Inspires and feeds and animates the whole.
> This active mind, infused through all the space,
> Unites and mingles with the mighty mass.
> Hence men and beasts the breath of life obtain,
> And birds of air, and monsters of the main,
> The ethereal vigour is in all the same,
> And every soul is filled with equal flame –
> As much as earthy limbs and gross allay
> Of mortal members subject to decay
> Blunt not the beams of heaven. . . .

After that, Anchises expounds the doctrine of the soul's purgation, and tells of the great cycle of birth, death, suffering, reincarnation: and after that he shows the pageant of the future, the glory and the mission of the sons of Rome. And yet, you know, the vision which began at Cumae with the picture of the boy who died because he flew too high ends, with the sorrow of the poet, and of all who loved Marcellus, for that other youth of noble promise, who died too soon. Here is the counterpoint of the whole poem: Arms and the Man . . . the walls of Rome . . . the Roman race; Icarus, Rome, Marcellus.

manibus date lilia plenis.

May I read you just a few more lines, this time from the version given us by my friend Mr. Day Lewis?[21] They are very different in effect from Dryden's lines, but they are also noble poetry and give us something of what Virgil meant.

The life-force of these seeds is fire, their source celestial,
But they are deadened and dimmed by the sinful bodies they live in –
The flesh that is laden with death, the anatomy of clay:
Whence these souls of ours feel fear, desire, grief, joy,
But encased in their blind dark prison discern not the heaven-light above
Yes, not even when the last flicker of life has left us,
Does evil, or the ills that flesh is heir to, quite
Relinquish our souls. . . .
Each of us finds in the next world his own level. . . .

(That is surely a very reticent and euphemistic way of treating *quisque suous patimur manes.* The meaning rather is, I think, 'We suffer, each of us, for being what wwe are.' But the rest is accurate and lovely) –

Each of us finds in the next world his own level: a few of us
Are later released to wander at will through broad Elysium,
The Happy Fields; until in the fullness of time, the ages
Have purged that ingrown stain, and nothing is left but pure
Ethereal sentience and the spirit's essential flame –

aetherium sensum atque aurai simplicis ignem.[22]

Shakespeare knew and loved that line, and that is why his Cleopatra, at the end, can say, when nothing else is left for her but suffering and love,

I am fire and air, my other elements
I give to baser life . . . Husband I come.

But what is, in effect, the answer given to Aeneas by his father?

All these souls when they have finished their thousand year cycle

God sends for. And they come in crowds to the river of Lethe
So that, you see, with memory washed out, they may revisit
The earth above and begin to wish to be born again. . . .[23]

The answer is, you see, that what inspires these souls is not 'a terrible craving' for the life of mortal men, but a wish for the next stage in a pilgrimage and a rebirth that brings them further on the road towards a perfect consummation, when all evil shall be purged away.

Virgil's doctrine isn't exactly ours, and how far Virgil thought of it as true in fact or only 'somehow like the truth,' no one can say. But I am sure that this initiation as a whole prepares the hero not simply for a mystical experience here or hereafter, but for life and work in Italy for Rome, as Rome should be, and therefore for us all.

Is it not true that Virgil's poetry speaks, as MacKail has said, of actual life directly to us, coming afresh to each generation, to each reader, as a revelation of the beauty of the world and the wonder of the human soul?

When Dante's Beatrice sent Virgil to the help of Dante, I am sure it was not simply because Virgil's style had kindled Dante's love for his own language and inspired his verse. Nor was it simply that in Virgil's praise of Rome and of the Roman race he found a prophecy, a prayer and an assurance of that Holy Roman Empire to which, hoping against hope, he looked for peace and justice in the world; nor even because Virgil was believed by him to be a prophet of the birth of Christ. Rather, I think, it was because each poet in his own way had discerned a clue, though not the answer, to the eternal mystery of life and death and joy and sorrow, and that clue somehow was found in thoughts of sacrifice as the condition of achievement, and love of which the price is pain. Homer, Virgil, Dante, let us remember all of them. They all are worth remembrance.

1. *Aen.* 6.664.
2. *Ibid.* 5-9.
3. *Ibid.* 37-9.
4. *Aen.* 1.456ff.
5. *Ibid.* 92-101.
6. *Aen.* 6.889.
7. *Aen.* 3.441-60.
8. See Professor H. E. Butler's Introduction and Notes. I have learnt much from his edition, but on points like these feel bound to differ from his view.
9. *Aen.* 6.103ff.
10. *Od.* 10.449ff.
11. *Od.* 11.141ff.
12. *Il.* 18.79-80.
13. *Il.* 16.7-10, *Aen.*, 2.724.
14. *Aen.*, 6.268.
15. *Ibid.* 314.
16. *Ibid.* 426ff.
17. See Professor H. E. Butler's edition, pp. 11-14.
18. *Aen.* 2.559-63.
19. *Aen.* 6.660ff.
20. *Il.* 24.110. The significance of this line was, among modern scholars, I believe, first discerned by the late Sir John Myres.
21. The *Aeneid* of Virgil, translated by C. Day Lewis, London, 1954.
22. *Aen.* 6.743-7.
23. *Ibid.* 748-51.

A Roman Post-Mortem:

An Inquest on the Fall of the Roman Republic

RONALD SYME

Coming among you in response to an amicable and flattering invitation, namely to deliver the third of the Todd Memorial Lectures, I cannot feel myself wholly among strangers. Nor, I trust, will the theme selected for the discourse be altogether remote and unfamiliar. The series which opened so auspiciously with the *Aristocratic Epoch in Latin Literature* and went on to *The Emperor and his Clients* announces a high standard for emulation – and it also counsels the choice of a subject that shall deal not with books and texts and words only, but with the behaviour of men and governments.

When a war has been lost, a political system overthrown or an empire shattered and dispersed, there is certain to be a post-mortem enquiry, and the discussion is seldom closed with the decease of the survivors: it may be perpetuated to distant ages, and, as strife is the father of all things, so is dispute and contention the soul of history. One of these great necrological argumentations is the fall of the Roman Empire in the West – a revolution, so the historian Gibbon pronounced, 'which will ever be remembered, and is still felt, by the nations of the earth.'

Another is the fall of the Roman Republic. Here the breach between the old and the new was not, it is true, so wide, and the damage was quickly repaired, with a stable order ensuing. The Republic had been far from Republican, and the new dispensation under the rule of Caesar Augustus was not wholly monarchical. Behind the political struggles in the last age of the Free State at Rome, and behind the story of wars and battles, can be discerned, as a steady process, the emergence of centralized government.

The process is intelligible, but the causes of it and the stages are a perpetual theme for diagnosis and debate among scholars and historians. Perhaps the time has come to go back and discover what the Romans themselves thought about the catastrophe. Who was to blame? There were plenty of survivors, and the last convulsion was recent indeed to the contemporaries of Caesar Augustus. It opened in the year 49 BC, when Julius Caesar, the proconsul of Gaul, invaded Italy, it went on through civil wars and the despotic government of the Triumvirate, and it closed in 31, when the last of the war-lords, Caesar's heir, was victorious at the Battle of Actium. Already in 28 and 27 BC the shape of the new order, the Principate, was receiving public and legal definition.

Yet it is not at all easy to recapture the tone and arguments of the debate. No single and explicit statement exists anywhere. The written history of the time has vanished utterly, no political speech survives, no pamphlet, no memoirs. Compared with what went before and what came after, the Age of Augustus acquires the paradoxical dignity of an obscure and highly controversial period. Recourse must be had to official documents – with due caution; to the Augustan poets – again with due caution. And silence itself will be revealing. Important truths are often awkward truths, to be covered and disguised, from fear, from complicity, or for comfort.

The inquest may now begin. After a political catastrophe, why not turn round and inculpate the political system? A facile escape. It was denied to the Romans. The Republic was the very essence of Rome, it had endured through five centuries. Senate and people broke the Samnites, defied Hannibal, the Carthaginians, and brought down the successors of Alexander in the kingdoms of the East. Greeks might assert primacy in the arts and sciences, but not in the art of government. They might appeal to the wisdom of ancient legislators. In vain: their inferiority was registered by the turbulence of their civic history, and not least by the suspicious consolation of political utopias. The Romans could assert a powerful counter-claim. Their constitution was created, not out of plan or theory, not by one man only, but by long generations and by the efforts of many statesmen.[1] Here in truth was the balanced and ideal commonwealth: to discern which was not beyond the power even of a Greek, if he travelled, learned practical wisdom – and discarded national conceit.

To indict the Republican system of government was not only painful and intolerable: at the most a Roman was prepared to recognize imperfections of detail, or the need for adjustments. Moreover, it argued a lack of courage and faith. Caesar Augustus had just restored the rule of Senate and people, taking for himself powers by delegation. Not King or Dictator, but Princeps.[2] For that act the First Citizen has been much praised, then and subsequently. The reasons that moved the master of the legions were not wholly sentimental or traditional. A legal definition of the supreme authority was attractive, indeed inevitable. It enabled Augustus to control and work the constitution more effectively, to check the ambitions of others, to canalize patronage, and to provide for the undisturbed transmission of the power.

The Republic being to the Romans both a necessary mechanism and a necessary way of thought, and therefore invulnerable, might not the recent calamities be put down to the fault of the governing class? What an opportunity for a rancorous democrat, what a theme for anger and invective! He might attack the aristocracy for their reckless ambition, careless of the commonwealth; he might arraign the shameless nepotism that protected and rewarded the feeblest members of their own order; he might denounce military incompetence, consigning thousands of Roman citizens to their deaths in the pursuit of glory and conquest; and he might round off the indictment with corruption, vice and rapacity.

How the thing could be done, a retired politician had recently demonstrated. The historian Sallust in his narration of the Conspiracy of Catilina launched a general attack upon the oligarchy that governed Rome in the last age of the Republic. His technique, varying but concentrated to one purpose, is instructive. Sulla, by victory in civil wars, by violence and by confiscation, brought the *nobilitas* back to power. Sulla is therefore regarded by Sallust as the author of all evil.[3] Catilina had been one of Sulla's men; the criminal ambitions of Catilina are made out to be a natural and inevitable product of the system that Sulla established.

But the historian has an even more damaging device. Cato was the firmest champion of that government, he waged a strong war in its defence against all subversive elements, and in the end he died for the Republic, achieving renown and consecration as a martyr in the cause of *Libertas*: Cato refused to submit to the victor in civil war, and preferred suicide to enslavement. Now Sallust in his monograph produces a speech by Cato in the Senate. It calls for the ultimate penalty against Catilina and his associates, and it carries a strong and bitter denunciation of sloth, greed and iniquity against that party of which Cato was himself one of the leaders.

Cato reminded his audience how Rome had grown great in ancient days through valour, integrity and justice; now, however, the State was poor and individuals were prosperous; the love of riches engendered the love of ease and luxury. Everything could be had for money or influence. Palaces and estates, wealth, possessions and works of art, all were dearer to their owners than was the Commonwealth.[4] Not only that. The conspiracy, in Cato's words, had been engineered by men of birth and family – *coniuravere nobilissimi cives.*[5]

And finally, the supreme condemnation of the aristocracy; not luxury or crime, but mediocrity. Sallust composes a tribute to the contrasted excellences of Cato and of Caesar. What is his justification? Because, he says, Cato and Caesar were the only truly great men at Rome in their age.[6]

Whether the aristocracy deserved so savage a handling might be doubted. There was still virtue and capacity in the old families – and no monopoly of honesty (very far from it) in the commercial classes. What, on a narrow and partisan estimate, is construed as luxury or corruption may yet be a manifestation of vitality; and the last age of the Republic with much turbulence, enjoyed freedom of speech and produced a great flowering of oratory and poetry. It might have been more equitable to absolve the governing class as a whole, to turn the edge of censure against a venal plebs, rapacious businessmen, the intrigues of bankers, the political apathy of the middle class in the towns of Italy – and the exorbitant ambitions of the generals.

Irrelevant, however, is the incrimination or exculpation of the aristocracy as a class. Privilege had always existed; it belonged to the natural order of things. If privilege was asserted and exploited by those on top, it was accepted and admired by those beneath.[7] Rome had gone through a revolutionary process. But none of the leaders of parties most active therein fought to change the structure of society – only to augment their own rank, wealth and power.

Nor could it have been expedient to attack or criticize the aristocracy under the new order of Caesar Augustus. The Revolution, now consolidated, was all for stability and conservation. Augustus for his ordering of the Roman State required not only the fabric of the Republic but the men and the families. They were to adorn the first ranks of the government, they were to act as leaders in society – and they were to be used in Augustus' own system of a monarchy that should be supported by an elaborate nexus of dynastic alliances in the aristocracy. In the civil wars he had fought against the *nobiles*. Victorious, and now a legitimate ruler, he became their friend and patron.

In the wars, the brave men and the loyal had perished, fighting in defence of the Republic against military despotism. Their names stand on record; but many of the most illustrious families in the Roman aristocracy are absent from the roll of honour of the Republic's dead. In fact, they survived the age of tribulation, and, for the most part, were ready to come to terms with the victor, for their mutual advantage.[8] What destroyed the *nobilitas* was not the wars of the Revolution but the murderous peace of the Caesars.

To the heirs of the *nobilitas*, the Roman people were pledged (so it was widely held) to pay a tribute in return for the great services of their ancestors.[9] The Emperor now came to replace the People as the source of honours. Augustus by control of the elections abated the dangerous excesses of open political competition, and, by favour, accorded to the *nobiles* a preferential treatment. He also subsidized them with money grants; and by his bounty he rescued from obscurity ancient houses of the aristocracy which through misfortune or incompetence had long ago fallen out of the race for honours and glory. Names never heard of for centuries now return to adorn the roll of the Republic's magistrates, and with the passage of a few years the new monarchy which grew out of the Revolution exhibits a strongly aristocratic complexion, patrician houses like Claudii, Valerii, Fabii, and Cornelii being prominent in the consulate.[10]

The *nobiles* might regain prestige, but not such power as before. They had once behaved in war and peace with all the pride and independence of clan-chieftains or barons. It was now intended that they should be useful as well as decorative. Moreover, they were not allowed a monopoly: they had to share privilege and station with the new men emergent from the Revolution, the adherents of Augustus promoted and enriched for loyalty and service.

If the aristocracy had to surrender much of its real power, and abate its ambitions, all the greater was the temptation to insist upon the show and the trappings, to advertise the claims of birth and pedigree. More so, perhaps, than in the last epoch of the Republic. And in those aspirations of the nobility the new men might easily concur. They had every reason to support and magnify that station and rank to which they had recently been admitted; they cheerfully adopted its pretensions and its prejudices. Social mimicry is the constant accompaniment of political success. Dual though it is in origin, the new aristocracy of the Empire pays homage to the same ideals.

Since the governing class as a whole, the past along with the present, was thus protected from attack, it would be necessary to look for individual culprits. Might not some of the political leaders be incriminated, for pride and ambition, for blunders or incompetence, for the fatal refusal to make concessions and adjustments?

Cato in his own life-time had incurred blame for that inflexible spirit (or noble obstinacy) which denied all compromise and sometimes appeared to harm the cause he was defending.[11] Moreover, Cato might deserve some share of responsibility for the clash of arms in which the Republic perished. Cato, it might have been said, was not merely a man of principle – he was stenacious and astute politician. If he came in the end to support Pompeius the Great against Caesar, it was not from illusions about Pompeius. His preference was tactical – to break Caesar first, then Pompeius, if it could be done.[12]

Cato failed. But Cato through defeat and suicide became a force more potent than ever in his life-time. There was hardly a Roman that could resist the spell.[13] Even his political enemies, such as Sallust, were quickly constrained to pay homage to his memory – and even Augustus could invoke Cato, in the interests of political stability and conservatism. Cato, it was said, preferred any government rather than none; and one of Cato's loyal followers proclaimed that even submitting to tyranny was better than civil war.[14] Now Augustus was of the opinion that it was better to have imperfect laws and abide by them than be always changing;[15] when asked his opinion of Cato, he had an answer: 'anybody who will not want the existing order to be altered is a good man and a good citizen';[16] and Augustus actually wrote a pamphlet on the subject of Cato.[17] The purpose and the argument do not lie beyond conjecture – a sermon on stable government.

Cato was dead and sanctified when Caesar's heir was making his debut as a military adventurer. Not so Brutus and Cassius. They were his sworn enemies. Augustus, for all his tolerance, good sense, or duplicity, could hardly have been expected to rehabilitate the memory of Brutus and Cassius. Those men had assassinated his adoptive parent, they had been duly condemned to death by a court of law. Nobody else, however, was debarred from extolling Brutus and Cassius. It was generally recognized that the cause for which Brutus and Cassius fought at Philippi was the better cause. The best men were there also: they, or their sons, avowed it proudly under the rule of Augustus.[18] Devotion to the memory of the Liberators had not yet become a symptom or a proof of disaffection with the rule of the Caesars.

There remains Cicero, who was killed when standing in defence of the Republic, but who was not regarded by Republicans quite as one of themselves, either then or in his posthumous reputation. The political career of the great orator was open to damaging criticism on various counts. More often, it is true, for compliance than for obstinacy. Yet if Cicero might seem by his end amply to have redeemed himself from earlier weaknesses, there might well be two opinions about the wisdom of a policy that invoked civil war in the defence of the Commonwealth: to destroy Marcus Antonius, Cicero in the last year of his life raised up the young man, Caesar's heir, an adventurer with a private army.

That young man, a few months later, was one of the three who signed the death-warrent of Cicero. A shameful act, but one among many such acts. What, then would be said or thought about Cicero when the era of the war was closed and Rome enjoyed concord and stability under the rule of Caesar Augustus? It was a delicate question then, and no single answer is now available.

Previously it had not been necessary to discredit the memory of Cicero (there was no Ciceronian party in Roman politics), the times changed quickly, and the contest for the supreme power with Marcus Antonius afforded (and required) more powerful weapons of propaganda. After the victory Cicero's memory was even less a political issue, and silence was the best remedy.[19]

But the name of that Roman who so excelled in oratory as to be a worthy rival to Demosthenes could not always be avoided; and the historian of the civil wars would have to pronounce a verdict somewhere. A fragment survives, preserving the obituary notice as composed by Livy. It is sympathetic but balanced. Except in his death, Cicero did not bear adverse fortune as a man should; and as for his death, he suffered only what he would have inflicted on others had he been victorious in the struggle.[20]

An anecdote is instructive. Plutarch tells how Augustus one day came upon one of his grandson reading a book of Cicero. The boy in dismay made fruitless attempts to conceal it. Augustus took the volume, stood there reading it for some time, and gave it back with the words: 'a great writer, and a great patriot'.[21]

The Princeps, it should seem, need not have confined his approbation within the walls of the palace. He could praise Cato if he chose, in the interests of ordered government: why not Cicero? Cicero was a champion of enlightened conservatism. There was much of value in his political thinking; and the ideal commonwealth which he depicted in the books *De Re Publica* drew its strength not from theory but from history, for it was nothing less than an exposition, with suitable embellishments (but no structural modification), of the Roman state in a past age of stability and felicity.[22]

That Caesar Augustus had recourse for guidance to the writings of Cicero, or to any writings, is not a convincing notion. That the phraseology employed by Cicero (and no doubt by many of Cicero's contemporaries) should recur in the Principate of Caesar Augustus can hardly prove anything more than the recurrence, in familiar and useful words, of political argumentation – and political deceit. The Augustan system took its origin from facts, not from books; its authors were politicians, diplomats and generals, not theorists.

So much for the political leaders on the Republican side. For one reason or another it was impossible to make scapegoats of Cato, of Brutus, of Cicero. Flagrant by contrast was the guilt of the military leaders who subverted the Commonwealth by their ambition and brought on the civil wars by their rivalries. In the opinion of Cato the trouble began, not when Caesar crossed the Rubicon but when, a dozen years earlier, Pompeius, Crassus and Caesar formed a compact to control the State.[23] That opinion found favour and support: Asinius Pollio adopted the year 60 BC for the beginning of his history.[24]

Yet the three dynasts were not totally or unreservedly to be condemned. They were men of splendour and power, they exhibited *virtus* and they pursued *gloria*. If they augmented the dominions of the Roman people, they would have to be honoured at Rome – and Augustus paid suitable and especial honour to his predecessors in that role.[25]

Of the three, Crassus failed in his war beyond the Euphrates, and so could properly be blamed for criminal aggression. But Pompeius and Caesar were resplendently successful in their conquests. Caesar was consecrated by the heir to his name, yet by paradox *'Divi filius'* when undisputed master of Rome seems to award the preference not to his parent but to Pompeius Magnus. The evidence is startling; it is consistent; and it comes from the three great writers of Augustan Rome that stand so close to the government – two poets and a historian.

In the Odes of Horace, Julius Caesar is not quite referred to as a person.[26] The *Aeneid* of Virgil is an epic poem devoted to the ultimate origins of Rome and the Julian House, highly symbolical and allegorical. Augustus is not only prefigured in Aeneas: he is revealed in three visions of the future. First, *The Promise of Jupiter*. To comfort Venus, the father of gods and men discloses the glory that is to be, its culmination in the young Caesar, conqueror of the nations to the world's end and a prince of peace.[27] Next, *The Shield of Aeneas*, with all Roman history portrayed as leading up to the victory of Rome and of Italy at Actium.[28] Thirdly, *The Revelation* of *Anchises*: the parent of Aeneas calls up before him in the lower world the muster roll of Aeneas' line and of the heroes of Rome, regal and Republican, down to '*Augustus Caesar divi genus*', who will establish the Golden Age in Italy.[29]

Where is Julius Caesar? The list passes from Romulus to Augustus, but he is nowhere to be found in that vicinity. Caesar is segregated, being introduced later, along with Pompeius. Both stand outside of the chronological order of Roman history, and neither is referred to by name. That is not the most remarkable thing. Anchises with solemn adjuration exhorts them both to refrain from civil war. Which shall disarm first? Not Pompeius but Caesar.[30]

The historian confirms the poet. For Livy it was a question whether the birth of Caesar were a greater blessing or a greater curse.[31] And Livy was so generous in his praise of Pompeius that Augustus called him a '*Pompeianus*'. That did not, we are told, in any way impair the friendship between emperor and historian.[32] On the contrary, these men understood each other. Livy was quite sincere; and the exaltation of Pompeius, so far from offending Caesar Augustus, fitted admirably with his policy.

Whatever was known and remembered about the acts and ambitions of Pompeius the Great could be passed over: in the end he had fallen at Pharsalus commanding the armies of the Republic against Caesar. Whereas Caesar (whatever the rights and wrongs of the dispute) began an accursed war by his invasion of Italy, and Caesar the

Dictator had been assassinated by honourable men.

It was expedient for Augustus to dissociate himself from Caesar: the one destroyed the Republic, the other restored it. How could that be done? Easily, and with the fairest pretext. Caesar had been deified, he was no longer a mortal man. When Caesar's heir himself died at the term of his long presidency of the Roman State, there were carried in the funeral procession the images of his ancestors, and also those of the great generals of the past. Pompeius Magnus was among them, but not Caesar.[33] The artifice of Augustus is patent. He exploited the divinity of his parent and paraded the titulature of *'Divi filius'*. For all else, Caesar the proconsul and dictator was better forgotten.

An authentic scapegoat has been identified. And there were others. Upon Octavianus' partners in the triumviral powers, Aemilius Lepidus and Marcus Antonius, might be laid the responsibility for the proscriptions, and notably upon Antonius the guilt of the murder of Cicero. For the rest, Lepidus was a flimsy character, rapidly discarded, and by his very insignificance at the same time removed from blame and unworthy of rehabilitation. Not so the great Antonius, the true author of the Caesarian victory at Philippi and the rival of Caesar's heir in the supreme struggle for the dominion of the world.

The war of words began before the armed decision at Actium, and it was prosecuted afterwards, with no less intensity. Not only was it Antonius' fault, the renewed civil war – for his rival (it was claimed) wanted only peace, concord and the restoration of Republican government. Not only criminal ambition, but criminal folly. Antonius had now become an oriental monarch, aspiring to subjugate Rome and Italy to foreign rule. His habits were alien, his armies, his allies – and the Queen of Egypt his wife, *'sequiturque (nefas) Aegyptia coniunx'*.[34]

The war as managed by Caesar's heir was a war solemnly

and legally declared against Egypt. If Antonius stood by Cleopatra, he was stamped as a traitor and consigned to infamy. And so it turned out. The legend of Actium is a familiar theme, lavishly exploited by the Augustan poets. After Caesar, Antonius is the second scapegoat, and much more satisfactory in the intensity of the emotion evoked, moral, patriotic and xenophobic.

None the less, the account is not closed when Caesar and Antonius are indicted. Attractive though it might be to single out one man (or two) for execration, and an easy solution for the vulgar and the superficial, a scrupulous enquirer or a thoughtful patriot would have to confess that the evil was deeper in its roots and more pervasive in its manifestations. Though it was hardly possible (as has been shown) to incriminate the whole governing class, they might share the guilt if it was nation-wide, and envisaged as moral and religious rather than political.

Through what sins and transgressions had the Roman People come so near to destruction? Various answers were available. An ancestral curse was working itself out: it originated in Troy, or at the founding of Rome when Romulus shed his brother's blood.[35] Or the national gods had been neglected, their sanctuaries crumbling in ruin.[36] Or the traditional ideals of morality and frugality had lapsed, generation after generation sinking deeper in luxury, crime and corruption.[37]

The nation's guilt and the urgent need for a reformation are most eloquently declared in certain odes of Horace, which herald and support the social programme of Caesar Augustus. How far that programme succeeded is a large question. A historian a century later expresses his doubts; according to Cornelius Tacitus, luxury was unbridled from the War of Actium down to the fall of Nero.[38]

Nor, be it noted, was the moral outlawry of Caesar and of Antonius maintained in all its rigour. After a few years, it seems, the anger and the fervour about Actium abated in the consciousness of stability and prosperity. And the family of the renegade subsisted as an element in the Caesarian dynasty. The daughters of Antonius were at the same time nieces of Augustus, and from this line came three emperors of Rome – Caligula, Claudius and Nero.

There were no personal and family causes of this nature to rehabilitate the memory of Caesar the Dictator. Justice was late in coming. As the years passed, however, the origins of the Empire could be seen in a proper perspective; and a historian might be inclined to replace Caesar in the series of the rulers of Rome, for various reasons, and especially if he were distrustful of Augustus and of Augustan valuations. Tacitus frequently refers to Caesar, and never with disrespect; and he is hostile to the idealization of Pompeius the Great.[39]

Such is the termination of the post-mortem, and not wholly conclusive. It provokes a further question. Was the corpse wholly defunct? If a man looked about him he might be impelled to doubt it, for he could see the outer fabric of the Republic intact, the old families back in office, and the old phrases back in currency. Much had altered, it is true, but not everything for the worse. Though everybody made haste to bury and cover up the twenty years of tribulation, the period had not in fact been an orgy of continuous destruction. There were not battles every year; and many of the battles had been decided with little bloodshed, through the well-timed treason of political generals or the mass capitulations of citizen soldiers. Even the standing armies, the savage taxation and the vast expropriations were not an unmixed evil: money circulated and energy was let loose.

Many of the profiteers of the wars became imperceptibly the profiteers of the peace. It is worth asking, which were the classes and regions to benefit from the centralized government that replaced the competitive anarchy of the Roman Republic? The answer can be briefly given.

The provincials gained protection from the master of Rome, and submitted to regular taxation in the place of arbitrary exactions. Caesar was also the patron of the urban poor, providing corn doles, and for some, allocations of land. The propertied class welcomed security and saw their estates rise in value. For business men the new régime held out new sources of investment, posts in the administration, and the prospect, if they wished it, of promotion into the senatorial order. As for the Senate itself, the lower members could now rise by merit or loyalty to the top, while the princes of the aristocracy, relieved from the expense and the dangers of competition for office, might qualify for the consulate by prerogative – through the patronage of Caesar Augustus.

However, not all men are ready frankly to acknowledge benefits conferred upon them. The Empire could be acclaimed by the provinces, the lower orders and by much of the middle class, commercial or landed. Not so easily by the aristocracy or by those who from tradition or snobbery were imbued by the same sentiments – or at least vocal in their expression.

The Empire needed no elaborate or sophistical justification to most classes and regions. Their feelings are known, or can be guessed. Imperial propaganda, as directed towards the inferior orders of society, might seem either superfluous or obvious and predictable. The upper classes needed a more subtle approach – or rather, it should be said, they gradually formulated the reasons and excuses for accepting the new order of things. How do men console themselves for the surrender of political freedom? With what arguments do they maintain that they have discovered the middle path, liberty without licence, discipline but not enslavement?[40] It would be an entertaining speculation, and not remote from the concern of the present age.

1. Such was the opinion of Cato the Censor, reproduced in Cicero, *De Re Publica* 2.2.

2. Tac. *Ann.* 1.9: 'non regno tamen neque dictatura sed principis nomine constitutam rem publicam.'

3. Sall. *Bell. Cat.* 11.4: 'sed postquam L. Sulla armis recepta re publica, bonis initiis malos eventus habuit,' etc.

4. *Ibid.* 52.5: 'sed per deos immortalis! vos ego appello, qui semper domos villas signa tabulas vostras pluris quam rem publicam fecistis'; *ibid.* 21f.: 'sed alia fuere quae illos magnos fecere, quae nobis nulla sunt, domi industria, foris iustum imperium, animus in consulendo liber, neque delicto neque lubidni obnoxius. pro his nos habemus luxuriam atque avaritiam, publice egestatem, privatim opulentiam; laudamus divitias, sequimur inertiam.'

5. *Ibid.* 24.

6. *Ibid.* 53.5: 'multis tempestatibus haud sane quisquam Romae virtute magnus fuit. sed memoria mea ingenti virtute, divorsis moribus fuere viri duo M. Cato et C. Caesar.'

7. Cic. *De. Re Pub.* 1.43: 'tamen ipsa aequabilitas est iniqua, cum habet nullos gradus dignitatis.' Pliny, *Epist.* 9.5.3.: 'nihil est ipsa aequalitate inaequalius.'

8. Tac. *Ann.* 1.2.: 'cum ferocissimi per acies aut proscriptione cecidissent, ceteri nobilium, quanto quis servitio promptior, opibus et honoribus extollerentur.'

9. Sen. *De Ben.* 4.30.4.: 'hic egregiis maioribus ortus est: qualiscumque est, sub umbra suorum lateat. ut loca sordida repercussu solis inlustrantur, ita inertes maiorum suorum luce resplendeant.'

10. To say nothing of a Furius Camillus after three and a half centuries, or a Quinctilius Varus descended from the nobility of Alba Longa.

11. Cic. *Att.* 2.1.8: 'nocet interdum rei publicae; dicit enim tamquam in Platonis πολιτείᾳ non tamquam in Romuli faece sententiam.'

12. Thus, when Pompeius was removed, Cato could prolong the struggle for *Libertas* against Caesar with a clear conscience. Cf. Lucan, *Phars.* 9.265f: 'unum Fortuna reliquit iam tribus e dominis.'

13. Compare the words of Velleius Paterculus, an ardent supporter of the Caesars (2.35.2): 'homo Virtuti simillimus et per

omnia ingenio diis quam hominibus propior.'

14. Plut *Pomp.* 54; *Brut.* 12.

15. Dio 53.10.1.

16. Mac. 2.4.8. 'quisquis praesentem statum civitatis commutari non volet, et civis et vir bonus est.'

17. Suet. *Aug.* 85.

18. Tac. *Ann.* 4.34: 'Messala Corvinus imperatorem suum Cassium praedicabat.'

19. Compare the opinion of Labienus, cited by the Elder Seneca (*Controv.* 10.3.6): 'optima civilis belli defensio oblivio est.'

20. Cited by the Elder Seneca (*Suas.* 6.22): 'omnium adversorum nihil ut viro dignum erat tulit praeter mortem, quae vere aestimanti minus indigna videri potuit quod a victore inimico ⟨nil⟩ crudelius passurus erat quam quod eiusdem fortunae compos victo fecisset.'

21. Plut. *Cic.* 12.

22. As surely emerges from statements in the tract itself, confirmed by *De Leg.* 3.4.12.

23. Plut. *Caes.* 13; *Pomp.* 47.

24. Hor. *Carm.* 2.1.1ff.:

> Motum ex Metello consule civicum
> bellique causas et vitia et modos
> ludumque Fortunae gravisque
> principum amicitias et arma
> nondum expiatis uncta cruoribus.

25. Suet. *Aug.* 31: 'proximum a dis immortalibus honorem memoriae ducum praestitit, qui imperium p.R. ex minimo maximum reddidissent.'

26. The nearest he can go is the 'Iulium sidus' of *Carm.* 1.12.47; the 'Caesaris ultor' of 1.2.44 is only a description of Augustus.

27. *Aen.* 1.286ff.:

> nascetur pulchra Troianus origine Caesar
> imperium Oceano, famam qui terminet astris,
> Iulius, a magno demissum nomen Iulo.
> hunc tu olim spoliis Orientis onustum
> accipies secura: vocabitur hic quoque votis.

28. *Aen.* 8.678f.:

> hinc Augustus agens Italos in proelia Caesar
> cum patribus populoque penatibus et magnis dis.

29. *Aen.* 6.789ff.:

hic Caesar et omnis Iuli
progenies magnum caeli ventura sub axem:
hic vir, hic est, tibi quem promitti saepius audis,
Augustus Caesar divi genus, aurea condet
saecula qui rursus Latio.

30. *Aen.* 6.832ff.:

ne, pueri, ne tanta animis adsuescite bella
neu patriae validas in viscera vertite viris;
tuque prior, tu parce, genus qui ducis Olympo,
proice tela manu, sanguis meus!

31. Sen. *Nat. Quaest.* 5.18.4: 'nam quod de Caesare maiori volgo dictatum est et a Tito Livio positum in incerto esse utrum illum nasci magis rei publicae profuerit an non nasci, dici etiam de ventis potest.'

32. Tac. *Ann.* 4.34: 'Titus Livius, eloquentiae ac fidei praeclarus in primis, Cn. Pompeium tantis laudibus tulit ut Pompeianum eum Augustus appellaret; neque id amicitiae eorum offecit.'

33. Dio 56.34.2f.

34. *Aen.* 8.685ff.:

hinc ope barbarica variisque Antonius armis,
victor ab Aurorae populis et litore rubro,
Aegyptum virisque Orientis et ultima secum
Bactra vehit, sequiturque (nefas) Aegyptia coniunx.

35. E.g. Virg. *Georg.* 1.501ff.: Hor. *Carm.* 3.3.21ff.

36. Hor. 3.6.1.ff.

37. *Ibid.* 46ff.

38. Tac. *Ann.* 3.55: (a digression following the speech in which Tiberius Caesar expressed a strong dislike for moral and sumptuary legislation).

39. Tac. *Hist.* 2.38: 'post quos Cn. Pompeius occultior non melior'; and, especially notable because of the context, which deals with the legislation of Augustus, *Ann.* 3.28: 'tum Cn. Pompeius tertium consul corrigendis moribus delectus, et gravior remediis quam delicta erant suarumque legum auctor idem ac subversor, quae armis tuebatur armis amisit.'

40. The formula is well attested, e.g. in the funeral oration upon Augustus (Dio 56.43.4), and in the words of Galba when adopting Piso as his successor (Tac. *Hist.* 1.16): 'neque enim hic, ut gentibus quae regnantur, certa dominorum domus et ceteri servi, sed imperaturus es hominibus qui nec totam servitutem pati possunt nec totam libertatem.'

The Emperor and His Clients

HAROLD MATTINGLY

I feel it a very great privilege to be here with you tonight to deliver the second Todd Memorial Lecture – a great privilege and a great pleasure. It has been a long way to come, and long ways, today, are hard ways. But we have a married daughter in New Zealand to draw us, and *Vicit iter durum pietas* ('Love has overcome the difficulties of the way'). But, just as Aeneas needed something beside his *pietas* to achieve the descent to the shades – his Golden Bough of Proserpine – so we too should hardly have made our journey 'Down Under' without our own Golden Bough, which in this case was your invitation to me to lecture.

The Todd Lecturer has to face the high standard set by the first lecturer, your own Professor Smith, and due to the great scholar whom the lecture was established to honour. He must try to give of his best, and he must try to find a theme of general human interest suited to the occasion. You will not wish to listen to subtleties of research, but will expect rather to have light thrown on the character and ways of the ancient Romans. My own lifework has been devoted to the study of the coinage of the Roman Empire, and, looking back on it, I think I have found a theme, which has become real to me after much labour, which is intensely human and which has an enduring interest for all who live in communities at all comparable with the Roman. In speaking to you of the Emperor and his clients I hope to help you to realise something of the character of the two sides in the great game of Empire – the governor and the governed.

In handling any particular class of evidence we must pause at times to take stock of its particular quality. It obviously makes a considerable difference whether your information is contained in historical writings, in oratory or poetry, or in official documents, such as inscriptions and coins. Such stocktaking is particularly essential in the case of the Roman Imperial coins; for, while they obviously have a message for the historian, it is not quite like any other message that he is called upon to decipher. It is only after nearly forty years of study that I seem to be able to focus them correctly and to see the broad facts as distinct from the countless problems of detail – in short, to distinguish the wood from the trees.

The Roman Imperial coinage attends the Empire during its whole course, reign by reign. It can usually be dated closely – often to a single year. It can usually be assigned with confidence to its mints, of which the capital, Rome, is naturally the chief. It provides us with a marvellous gallery of portraits, with the fullest possible record of the different styles and legends of the Emperors, with pregnant references to events, familiar in history, and with a steady commentary on those events and the policies centered on them. Above all, it is continuous. It takes us out of set periods and keeps us in touch with the Empire along its whole course, and it is the only surviving source that does so. Therein lies its great, its unique, value for the student.

The Roman coins obviously serve purposes beyond those of a mere medium of exchange. They are used in fact for publicity and propaganda. The first question we have to ask – and, if possible, answer – is this: were the authorities fully aware of these extra functions of coinage, and, if so, how seriously did they regard them?

The answer is quite definite and sure. The authorities were fully aware of them and regarded them with deep seriousness. The more one studies the Imperial coinage, the more convinced does one become of its essential earnestness. Publicity was not so readily attained by an age that had no cheap press and no radio. Propaganda is always important, and for propaganda publicity is necessary. The coin was issued steadily and passed freely from hand to hand. When the types were not fixed for long periods, but changed from year to year, men must have spent some little time in studying the coins which they carried in their pockets. They might even do so today, if we began to treat our coinage in the old – the medallic – way.

Every new Emperor was quick to make his features and titles familiar to his world. He carefully selected those events on which he wished the public to dwell, and adroitly suggested the interpretations which were to be placed upon them. If we attempt to find meanings in types of a character, seemingly general and colourless, we may be guilty of an occasional mistake of false emphasis. But we are certain to err more seriously, if, because of this risk, we neglect the task of interpretation altogether. In his stock of symbolical types – gods, virtues, buildings, animate and inanimate objects – the Roman mint-master had an instrument ready to his hand which could be applied to every changing occasion. Descriptive legends could be brought in to make the meaning more precise. Especially could the virtues of an emperor be used to paint a picture of the policy of a reign. By honouring the spirits that inspire an emperor you make plain the principles on which he is preparing to govern.

Let no one imagine that coin types were selected haphazard – that the particular choice of events to be illustrated and of the colours in which to paint them was left to subordinate officals of the mint. If we ask at what level the main decisions about the work of the mint was taken the coinage itself supplies a ready answer. It must have been at a very high one. No Emperor who took his duties seriously can have failed to give very serious thought to the messages that his coinage was to carry abroad into the world. If he was so neglectful, he was allowing a most powerful weapon of propaganda to slip out of his own hands into the hands of others who might use it to his disadvantage. Trajan, when he handed the dagger of office to his praetorian prefect, bade him use it 'for me, if I deserve it; if not, against me!' The emperor who gave his mint-master a free hand with the coinage would have been practising a similar self-denial, with far less sound reason or justification. Some Emperors, no doubt, *did* leave it to subordinates to make important decisions for them. But, with the mint, the neglect certainly never went very far down. It would be hard to point to any one period in the Empire when subordinate officals were left free to interpret in the coinage the intentions of the Government.

The coins of the Empire fall into two main series: the gold and silver issued by the Emperor, and the bronze and copper – subordinate token coinage – issued by the Senate. The mark of senatorial control (S. C. – *Senatus Consulto*) is as normally present on the token coinage as it is absent from the precious metals. But it is becoming every day more plain that the distinction is rather one of form than of final intention. The Emperor elected to give his arrangements for the token coinage the stamp of official approval in the Senate, but he never let the control of it pass out of his own hands. That is why we find such coinage with the mark S. C. even in imperial provinces like Gaul or Syria. It is quite inconceivable that the Emperor should have risked having propaganda, in a sense contrary to his own, put abroad by an independent Senate. It would have been seriously confusing to the public, and it might so easily have become dangerous to the Emperor himself. For, while the Empire could be seen to bear the stamp of eternity, the individual Emperor and dynasty were subject to the vicissitudes of fortune. There was indeed a dyarchy of a kind, a dual government by Emperor and by Senate. But the distinction was really no more than that of two ways in which the Emperor could proceed, with his self-chosen adviser, or in partnership with the Senate as representative of the Roman State – S.P.Q.R. (*Senatus populusque Romanus*). The only business transacted by the Senate alone was of subordinate importance.

To whom were the messages of the Imperial coinage addressed? And in what capacity did the Emperor address them? Nominally, of course, to the whole world, to the subjects of the Empire at large, as becomes evident when we hear of the *Salus generis humani* or the *Restitutor orbis terrarum*. Sometimes the message is directed to a particular section – senate, knights, people, army or provinces. But as a general rule we have to think of the *populus Romanus*, the great body of Roman citizens, as the audience in view, and in particular of the Roman citizens assembled in the city of Rome. We do not always appraise at its true value the importance of the Roman mob in its corporate capacity. The Empire, once founded, must continue to stand, for there was really no possible alternative. But while the Empire remained, Emperors might come and go. An Emperor must be sure where he stood. The first requirement was the support of the army – in particular of the praetorians of Rome. Hardly second in importance was the approval of the Senate, which alone could make Empire constitutional. But, however true it is that a government stands by force and constitutional precedent, it will always need the backing of public opinion if it is to enjoy any ease or security. Individually the Roman citizen had little power or freedom left him. He was quite at the mercy of an irrepressible autocracy if he chose to cross its path. But when he assembled in his myriads in amphitheatre or circus, or to cheer the Emperor on his arrivals and departures, he could express collectively what he dared not say individually. It was extremely dangerous for an Emperor to allow such public demonstrations to remain consistently unfriendly, and it was far from safe to suppress them by violence. Disapproval of the Emperor expressed in public gatherings might well be the prelude to his fall. Discontent might spread from those who could not give immediate effect to it to those who could – to the praetorian guard or the provincial armies. The course of obvious wisdom was to make full use of conciliation and material inducements to ensure that the vote of Rome, the central constituency of the Empire, should be heard in support of, not in denunciation of, its lawful ruler. Septimius Severus was seriously worried when the crowds in the amphitheatre greeted him on his return from the East to fight his rival Albinus, with cries of 'How long are we to be treated like this? How long are we to be kept at war?' And there is one more point. We often think of the mob of Rome as mercenary and servile – and not without justice. But we need also to think of the sounder elements, the *populus integer* as Tacitus calls them, which could often evince their independence and courage. The Roman masses sometimes showed a surprising tenderness – as when they protested, under Nero, against the execution of the savage rule that, when a master was killed, all slaves present on the premises at the time were liable to the death penalty – and an equally surprising courage, as when they, unlike the cringing Senate, disdained the threats and bribes of Didius Julianus and called on the provincial armies and their generals to vindicate the majesty of Rome, insulted by an Emperor who condoned the lawless murder of his predecessor and bought the Empire at infamous auction.

On the coinage, then, the Emperor spoke with set purpose to his subjects. It was not, of course, his only means of communications with them. He might deal with them individually, through the petitions bureau, the '*A libellis,*' or collectively by edicts. There were also the 'Acta Diurna,' a short summary of events, officially edited, and the 'Acta Senatus,' which, like Hansard, will only have interested a small and rather special public. But all these other forms have vanished, leaving barely a trace. The coins survive intact.

In what capacity would the Emperor speak to his Romans? He had so many parts to play that it is often difficult to decide in what particular guise he is appearing on any one occasion. To the army he was 'Imperator,' Commander-in-Chief. To the Senate he was 'Chief,' chief citizen (*princeps*) and chief Senator (*princeps senatus*). To the provincials he was the great ruler, with a power more than regal, though officially he lacked the name of king; the Greek East found no difficulty in calling him Βασιλεύς. To the flatterers and to some honest, simple-minded people he was a god. To his slaves and freedmen, and again to some servile folk, he was lord and master. To the Roman people he, as holder of the tribunician power, was their traditional representative and protector. In religion he was *pontifex maximus*, chief priest. But we have still to find some more general conception, in which all these aspects may be summed up. *Imperator, tribunicia potestate, pontifex maximus*, all describe some facets of the

Emperor's power, but he remains, in all the uniqueness of his position, one. The Romans tried to express this when they described him, unofficially, as *princeps*, No. I in the State, or, officially, as *Augustus*, 'the revered' – a title not actually of a god, but bordering on the divine sphere.

The Emperor possesses, by common consent, a unique power of initiative, *auctoritas*, based on his character, his descent and his position in Rome. Men always look to him to give them the lead. He is the one powerful man in front of a mass of humble subordinates. This relationship could find a tenderer expression in that of a father to his children, peculiarly agreeable to the Roman mind, with its immense veneration for the *patria potestas*. Augustus, after many years of rule, was acclaimed in the Senate 'Father of his country,' and he regarded this honour as the very crown of his career. Succeeding Emperors usually received the title, sometimes deferred for a time, until they had 'earned' it. With the idea of fatherhood was bound up that of 'saviour of the country,' expressed by the type of the civic-wreath, with the legend 'SPQR PP OB CIVES SERVATOS.' The wreath had originally been given as a kind of Victoria Cross, a reward of valour for the soldier who saved a comrade's life in action. Now the father-emperor 'saved' in a wider sense – sometimes, as was once cynically remarked, by not taking the lives that lay in his hands.

But, while the thought of the fatherhood of the Emperor was always somewhere in the background, ready to be called into application at need, there was another interpretation, always possible, on which it could be grafted. The Emperor was the *patronus*, the man of influence, might and wealth, who extended his protection, his *fides*, to the mass of small men who were his 'clients.' These 'clients,' the Roman people, gave him their own *fides*, their loyalty and service, in return. *Fides* is one of those two-way Roman words that cannot be rendered by any single word in English. The idea of good faith is always at its root, but the shade of meaning is determined by the quality of the person to whom it is applied.

The relationship of patron to client goes right back to the beginnings of Roman history. The patricians of the early Republic, in their fight with the plebs, depended on the support of the many clients whose interests were bound up with their own. The relationship is not so much to the fore in the later history, but we should do wrong to assume that it had lost its validity, because its immediate influence in politics is not so obvious. In the civil wars between Antony and Octavian there were Italian cities in the *clientela* of Antony that asked, for that reason, to be left out of the *coniuratio*, the solemn covenant sworn by Italy against him, and Octavian did not attempt to coerce them. The relation between patron and client was regarded as very close and very sacred, not far behind that of father and son. To wrong a client was a grave offence against *pietas*, right conduct. Duty to a client ranked above all except those to the nearest of kin. The Romans, in fact, found it natural to bridge social gulfs by this convenient relationship and to consecrate it by the most solemn symbols and associations. Under the Empire, it is true, the client might seem to have sunk to a very mean position. In Martial, the Roman writer of epigrams, he seems to be doomed to render petty services for trivial payments. But the reason for this is not far to seek. The relationship of patron and client was by no means forgotten, but it was now the Emperor who was the great patron, before whose splendour all lesser greatness paled, and the whole Roman people were his clients. He was not disposed to tolerate any too powerful patrons beside himself.

It is as patron to clients, then, that the Emperor speaks to his Romans, and of all the many forms in which he addressed them the coins are the only ones that have survived, in anything but fragments, today. The coins give us something like a continuous series of addresses by the Emperor to his clients. To understand them we have to realise the character and condition of the Emperor who issued them. We have also to imagine for ourselves the kind of needs and wishes that were met by them; the sort of response that they evoked. In a little book entitled 'The Man in the Roman Street' I have tried to picture the quality of the minds to which they were addressed. But we have still more to do if we are to understand them aright. We have to learn how to expand them and recover from them something of the fuller form, which they in their shorthand represent. The coins, we may suppose, show the Emperor accompanied by Valour and crowned by Victory, sacrificing in front of a temple. This must be expanded in some way like this: 'Since, by the power of valour in him, the Emperor has triumphed over the national enemy, he is now paying his vows, on behalf of himself and the State, to the gods who preserve the Empire.' In a similar way we have to expand the types themselves, to catch from the coins some glimpses of that world of larger art, which, except for rare survivals, has vanished. We have to imagine for ourselves the arches, the temples, the altars, the great groups of statuary or painting, of which all record would have been lost if the Roman government had not had the foresight to insert short mention of them in the Imperial coinage. The few that actually survive will help us to reconstruct the many that were lost.

Out of the immense field that opens up before us – nothing less than the survey, under a particular aspect, of the whole of Roman Imperial history – we can obviously only select a few items for full discussion tonight. First and foremost come the *panis et circenses* (bread and the circus-races), which according to the Roman satirist Juvenal, were all that the Roman people, once arbiter of peace and war, any longer cared for. Bread was a very near concern of the whole Roman people. The poor received their corn, issued free on ticket. But all classes wanted corn to be plentiful and cheap, and Rome, even assisted by Italy, was no more able to support herself. The overseas provinces – Africa and Egypt foremost, in a lesser degree Sicily and Sardinia – were regularly called upon for aid; and the Emperor maintained great corn-fleets to deliver the precious cargoes to the Italian ports. Prolonged bad weather might bring Rome near famine; for no great supplies were regularly stored. Nothing could so quickly render an Emperor unpopular as a failure of the corn supply. Claudius on one such occasion was pelted with crusts by an angry mob. The Emperors, therefore, strained every nerve to maintain a cheap and regular supply, and were never tried of advertising their efforts on the coins. They showed the corn goddess Ceres and her attendant spirit Annona; or Annona holding a statuette of Aequitas, the goddess of right measure; or Annona with the lighthouse of Alexandria beside her; or Annona with a captain, *navicularius*, in front of her. When the corn supply from Egypt was being cut off by Vespasian, Vitellius had himself represented in arms in its defence. Nero placed on his coins a plan of the port of Ostia, rebuilt by himself and Claudius. Commodus, who built a new African corn-fleet, celebrates his 'providence' by types of merchant ship and of himself as Hercules, greeted by Africa, who wears her elephant's skin headdress. The *modius* (corn-basket) of Nerva commemorates special arrangements that he made for the supply of corn to the Roman plebs. Hadrian's legend, *Tellus Stabilita*, with agricultural types, speaks in more general terms of the setting of agriculture throughout the Empire on a sure basis.

The supply of bread was not the only material favour that the Emperor conferred on the Romans. At accession, and on special occasions of rejoicing, at intervals throughout his reign, he would make a present of money – usually about seventy-five denarii (£3) – to all Romans. Such occasions were normally advertised on the coinage, either by the type of the goddess Liberalitas, holding her account-board and her horn of plenty, or by the scene of distribution, with the Emperor himself presiding over the beginning of the largesse. These bounties were not as unwarranted and demoralising as they might at first appear; they tended to encourage, and were meant to encourage, the rearing of larger families, the *Spes P. R.*, or hope of the race, to use the Roman phrase. Nerva and Trajan were the first to make special arrangements for orphan children out of the income derived from estates, mortgaged to Italian farmers. These *Alimenta Italiae* were celebrated by Trajan with the type of mother and child before the Emperor throned, or of the Emperor standing with his wards before him. A sestertius of Hadrian, showing the former of those two types, but with legend *Libertas restituta*, may refer to the same occasion; for the conception of 'liberty' under the Empire was an odd one – it might mean the right to receive Imperial favours as a citizen – and the Romans, ever fond of puns, often made play with he three words *Libertas, Liberalitas* and *Liberi* (children). Antoninus Pius, in honour of his wife Faustina the Elder, who was consecrated after her death in AD 140, founded the *puellae Faustinianae* (the girls of Faustina) in her honour. A fine aureus in the British Museum shows the Emperor dictating the charter to his secretary, behind whom is Faustina, leaning forward to advise; on a lower register stand the children and their nurses. At other times the Imperial indulgence took the form of a relief of burdens, such as the lifting of the expenses of the Imperial post from Italy, or the burning of bonds of old debts by a lictor in the forum under Hadrian. As benefactor in general the Emperor might be acclaimed as *restitutor* (restorer), with his protegée, a province or the whole world, kneeling before him waiting to be raised to her feet.

After material benefits come popular amusements, *circenses* after *panis*. The races in the circus themselves, a mad passion of Imperial Rome, which divided into furious factions over them, never appear on the coins, though they are freely celebrated by racehorses and their riders on the round coin-like discs with turned-up edges, the 'contorniates' of the fourth and fifth centuries. The Circus Maximus itself is shown on sestertii of Trajan, Caracalla and Gordian III and on an aureus of Septimius Severus – all four of them Emperors who improved or rebuilt it. The Colosseum, the gigantic creation of Vespasian and Titus, appears once on a sestertius of the latter ruler. The gladiatorial shows, that terrible passion of the Roman mob, are never mentioned on the coins. A decent reticence seems to forbid a public advertisement of an amusement of which many Romans were secretly ashamed, though they might think it necessary to maintain Roman valour. Wild beast shows were more liberally treated. Domitian, the first to exhibit a rhinoceros in Rome, placed it on a bronze coin. Antoninus Pius similarly showed an elephant, a much more familiar beast, but one particularly reserved for Imperial use. In AD 248, on the thousandth anniversary of Rome, Philip I exhibited for the public delight a whole series of beasts – lion, hippopotamus, goat, stag, elk, antelope – not omitting the she-wolf and twins – the latter presumably in effigy. Septimius and Caracalla contrived a wonderful ship, the sides of which suddenly opened and discharged a string of beasts – lions, tigers, bulls, ostriches, etc. With these shows we may perhaps class the Roman triumph, the great parade at which the victorious Roman general, accompanied by cheering soldiers, led his captives through the streets of Rome to the temple of Jupiter, Best and Greatest. General references to public merry-making, *Laetitia* or *Hilaritas*, were frequent. Rome had become a vast pleasure resort. The number of days devoted every year to games and festivals, in honour of the gods and in celebration of victories and anniversaries, was continually increasing until it added up to something near one in two. The pampered people of Rome enjoyed not only cheap victuals, but amusement free of cost at the expense of the rest of the world. The Emperor as giver of shows was naturally popular. It was not everyone who would stop to reflect that he need not be grateful to the particular giver, as every successor would have to do the same. But it was not a noble side of Roman civilisation. The finer artistic pleasures were not well catered for. The legitimate theatre was in decline, while vulgar displays of mime and pantomime ever gained at its expense. Athletic games were never popular in Rome. The desperate excitements of the dangerous races in the circus, the blood lust of the arena degraded and cloyed the Roman taste.

Like most potentates of all times, the Emperors were great builders. As we have seen, they created the Colosseum and restored the Circus; they dedicated new temples to the gods and repaired the old. They commemorated their victories by triumphal arches and columns. They beautified the city with many a forum and basilica. Many such buildings are recorded on coins, and in some cases the coin record is absolutely all that survives to give us an idea of lost greatness. Let us glance at a few that are thus recorded: the forum and column of Trajan, the Basilica Ulpia of the same Emperor, the arch of Trajan, the temple of Concord, the temple of Divus Augustus, the temple of Peace and many more. Trajan, in particular, was never weary of building; when he had nothing new to make, he restored other men's work. The wits said that his name was like the weed that grows everywhere on walls. The Colossus which stood in front of the Golden House, showing Nero as sun-god, was transferred to a new site by Titus; it is represented on a coin of the latter. Rome had always been famous for her aqueducts, and the Emperors Claudius and Trajan constructed new ones. Trajan represented his by a figure reclining on a rock, resting his elbow on an urn. The public roads of Italy were another pride of the Romans. Augustus had repaired them at his own expense. and Trajan added a new one, the Via Traiana, and represented it by a figure reclining on a rock and holding a wheel. Nerva, as we have seen, took the burden of the state-post in Italy on to the shoulders of his fiscus.

Many imperial occasions were made excuses for pageantry. The arrivals and departures of the Emperor were celebrated with much pomp and display. Crowds would assemble along the route and throw flowers, while the Emperor on horseback acknowledged their plaudits by raising his right hand. Symbolically, arrival and departure were represented by types of the Emperor riding, with or without attendant soldiers; arrival could also be represented by Rome welcoming the Emperor or presenting him to the Senate, or by Fortuna, the Home-bringer, greeting him. There would also be occasions when the Emperor would harangue his people; one such is represented on a sestertius of Hadrian. The Emperor stands on the *rostra* in front of a temple, and both he and the crowd raise their right hands.

Somewhere between pure religion and public entertainments come the *Ludi Saeculares*, an old festival of Etruscan origin, of purification and thanksgiving at the end of one age and the beginning of another. The age was reckoned at one hundred and ten years, a little beyond the extreme term of human life. Actually, the games were held at rather irregular intervals – in 17 BC by Augustus, in AD 88 by Domitian, in AD 204 by Septimius Severus. The games so celebrated by Claudius in AD 47-8 were really of a different order, as they commemorated the eight-hundredth year of Rome. So, too, Antoninus Pius celebrated the nine-hundredth year and Philip I the thousandth. The games of Augustus, Domitian, and Septimius Severus were all recorded on the coins, so fully, in their sum, that almost every feature finds illustration. Augustus showed the herald who called the people to games that 'no living man had seen or would see again,' and the issue of purifying elements (*suffimenta*) to the people. Domitian, on a fine series of sestertii, represented the Emperor receiving the gifts of natural produce (*fruges*) from the people, the prayer to Juno, dictated by him to the kneeling matrons, the procession of boys and girls singing the hymn to Apollo and Diana, the nocturnal sacrifices to Mother Earth and the goddesses of birth. Septimius Severus made a special place of honour for Hercules and Liber (Bacchus), the chief deities of his native city, Leptis Magna; he regarded them as his *di auspices*, who prompted and blessed all his endeavours. His coin type shows them standing side by side. They must have had a large place in the hymn of his year; but, alas, only inconsiderable fragments of it survive.

Religion played a great part in the public life of the Romans, who were regarded by the ancient world as 'the most religious of peoples.' Interest in religion had undoubtedly declined in the general decay of the Roman Republic, but there was a definite revival, partly spontaneous, partly helped by Augustus, at the beginning of the Empire. As time went on, interest in religion grew rather than declined. The third century, to say nothing of the fourth, was certainly an age of faith. The religious direction shifted as Eastern cults pressed in beside the old

Roman and Greek, but the spirit was still the same. More and more the Emperor emphasised his own position as Chief Priest and the parts played by his wife and children in the official religion. Men obviously felt that the continued welfare of Rome depended not only on the valour and initiative of its own Emperors, but even more on their *pietas*, their correct performance of the rights due to the gods of the State. The gods come more and more to be associated with the person of the Emperor and his family, as their patterns, their companions and their preservers (*comites, conservatores*). If you ever have any doubt of the persistence of ancient religion, if you have been led to suppose that paganism was moribund at the beginning of our era, study the series of Imperial coins. They are full of references to the gods and their worship, their temples and their altars. There is no possibility of hypocrisy or deception here. The emperors spoke in that language because it was the one that appealed directly to the hearts of their subjects.

There are two features of imperial religion that deserve special attention – the imperial vows and the worship of the deified emperors. The prayer most natural to the Roman was the vow (*votum*), a petition for a favour accompanied by a promise to pay for it by sacrifice when granted. Such prayers were being continually undertaken and paid (*suscepta* and *soluta*) by private individuals. They also formed the main part of the religious life of the community. On January 3rd in each year, the day of the vows (*votis*), vows were undertaken for the safety of the Emperor and his people. They were repeated, with special emphasis and impressive ceremony, at the end of longer terms of five or ten years (*vota quinquennalia* and *decennalia*) and with them were associated great public rejoicing and games, and often special imperial favours or announcements of policy. There would also be vows for such occasions as the departure of the Emperor and births or weddings in the Imperial family. The most common type of the vows is that of the Emperor sacrificing, dropping a few grains of incense on the altar when he formulates (*nuncupat*) his vows, but with patera in hand and *victimarius* and victim at his side as he pays them. The Emperor is, of course, only the focal point of a large and impressive scene, some details of which are occasionally shown on the coins – officers in attendance, harpists and flute-players and temple in the background. Sometimes it is the Roman State that is represented in sacrifice – the *Genius* of the Senate, an old man wearing the toga and carrying a sceptre, and the *Genius* of the Roman people, a young man bare to the waist, holding the horn of plenty. Other types, such as *Genius* or *Salus*, were often, though not invariably, associated with the vows.

The ancient East had always worshipped its rulers, or at least had placed them very near the gods. The habit had been generally adopted by the Greeks, after Alexander the Great. The Successor Kings were commonly honoured as 'Saviours,' 'Benefactors,' 'Gods' or 'Gods Manifest.' The boundary line between human and divine was well-nigh obliterated. Either the view was taken that deity was something that man could attain by conspicuous merit or service, as Hercules, Bacchus, Castor and Pollux had once attained it. According to one writer, Euhemerus, all the gods, even Jupiter himself, had once been great kings, who had ruled in power and glory on earth and after death had won Heaven by their virtues. Or else the divine element in the soul of the outstanding individual was recognized by worship of the divine powers and energies ('the Virtues') that find expression in him. What view was to be taken of the Roman Emperor, so great in fact, so beneficent in men's faith and hope? The Romans had learned about the deification of men from the Greek East, which had insisted on worshipping the 'Virtues' of its governors. Lucky it if it could find them! But the Roman had a rooted objection to the direct worship of a man as god: it offended his dignity and his common sense. But he was accustomed to regard all the dead as in some sense divine (*di manes*), and so a compromise was reached, by which Roman susceptibilities could be respected and yet due heed could be paid to the unique position of the Emperor. Outside Rome the Emperor was worshipped, even in his lifetime, as a god; in Rome, worship was only paid to his spirit (*Genius*) and his Virtues. But, once dead, if his memory was blessed by the Senate, he was consecrated, admitted to the heaven of the stars as a god (*Divus*) and honoured with a special guild of priests, a high priest or *Flamen* at their head, with altars, statues and temples. If the judgment of the Senate was unfavourable, the Emperor's acts were annulled and he was, so to speak, sent to Hell. In a few cases, the question of merit was left undecided and the Emperor remained in a sort of limbo. Not only emperors, but their near relatives – wives, fathers, sons and daughters – might be consecrated, and a new Pantheon of imperial deities came into being. This cult might prove a rallying point for imperial loyalty. Trajan Decius made it the centre of his pagan reaction, which aimed at restoring Roman valour, but which involved, as one of its consequences, the first persecution general of the Christian Church.

The *Divus* was translated from earth to Heaven. The eagle might be the symbol of his ascent, or it might actually bear him aloft. The coins show the figures of the *Divi* and *Divae*, the priests, altars and temples of their cult, the funeral pyre at which the eagle was liberated, the sacred throne (*pulvinar*) on which their attributes were set out, the image, borne on a car of elephants in the great public parade of the circus (*pompa circensis*). Immortality was usually associated with the upper air and the stars. A star might symbolise a new god, or he might be shown throned in heavenly majesty. Faustina the Younger is represented seated among the dancing Hours, or driving, like the moon-goddess, in her nightly chariot (*Sideribus Recepta*). The Roman people were familiar with this world of thought and symbolism and were constantly being reminded of it on the coins. Vows were paid to the *Divi*, and some simple souls seem actually to have believed that they were cosmic powers, capable of influencing the physical world. Poets and artists strained their ingenuity to elaborate the theme. Statius, a court poet of Domitian, picutres the stars of the Flavian heaven playing by night on the head of Domitian on his great equestrian statue in the Forum. Even hard-headed men of affairs, like the elder Pliny, accepted the idea of consecration as the substance of a plain truth – that the Emperor who rightly performed his duty of helping his fellow men thereby passed out of the ranks of ordinary mortals, whose memory dies with them. With the coming of Christianity the worship of the god-man had to go, though traces of it lingered on to the death of Theodosius the Great. But the old sentiment found new forms. The Christian Emperor was venerated as the chosen of God, crowned by His hand. His passing might be likened to that of Elijah, caught up to Heaven in the chariot of fire. The form has changed, but the feeling abides.

There were, as we have seen, occasions when the Emperor addressed his appeals to particular classes – to the Senate, to the knights, or to the Roman people – praising his concord with the Senate, linking his heir as 'prince of the youth' to the knights, promising favours to the Roman people. Occasionally, too, he spoke directly to his provinces or even to the whole Roman world. But there was one class that stood in a very special relation to the Emperor, and that was the Roman army. The Roman legionaries were, of course, Roman citizens and, as such, members of the general body of imperial clients. But, as soldiers, they entered into a special bond with the Emperor, which ranked even higher than that of client and patron. They swore allegiance directly to him ('swore into his words,' as the Romans put it), hailed him as Emperor (*Imperator*), and entered into the special relationship of military loyalty to him. In return for their allegiance they received their pay – which rose at intervals through the Empire – their pensions on discharge, their military decorations, their special privileges and, perhaps most important of all, the exceptional gift, the donative, given at accession and other rare occasions. The army was too important a part of the State to be kept out of the public records. Victories in the field were freely celebrated. Appeals were often made to the 'Harmony and Loyalty' (*Concordia* and *Fides*) of the troops. Be it noted that the emphasis on these desirable qualities often cloaked secret misgivings. *Fides Militum* might almost be described as the watchword of the terrible military anarchy of the third century, when Emperor after Emperor was murdered by his 'faithful comrades.' The Emperor is often shown haranguing his men, leading them into the field or receiving their plaudits as victor. But the peculiar relation of the Emperor to his troops was always kept as one of the Imperial secrets, the *arcana imperii* – if not an absolute mystery, at least one of the things about which you did not talk a great deal in public. The donatives, to take a special case, were never recorded on the coins; largesses to the people invariably, donatives never. Emperors from Septimius Severus onwards seem to have met these special and heavy charges out of their Private Fund, the *Res privata.* That was what Septimius meant on his deathbed when he exhorted his sons 'to be of one mind with one another, to enrich the soldiers, and to despise the rest of the world'! It was out of confiscations that the Private despise the rest of the world'! It was out of confiscations that the Private Fund was mainly fed. There were two reasons for this unwillingness to advertise a necessity of empire which, while naturally acceptable to the soldiers, could be very irksome to the Emperor who had to find the money. One was that the giving of donatives was part of the confidential relationship of the commander-in-chief with his men, a private matter between fixing the rewards of his troops; it was only after deducting them from the yield fixing the rewards of his troops; it was only after deducting them from the yeild expenses. The other reason was their extravagant scale. Marcus Aurelius and Lucius Verus actually gave 20,000 sesterii (about £200) to each praetorian. Didius Verus actually gave 20,000 sesterii (about £200) to each praetorian. Didius Julianus, who bought the empire at auction, gave 25,000 sestertii (£250). The legionaries got their share, perhaps helf that of the praetorians. This scale, so vastly above that of the largesse of about 300 sestertii (£3) a head, was likely to provoke bitter comment if advertised. It was enough if the burden was recognised as a bitter necessity and left as such. In the last resort, the Empire rested on force; only the master of the guard and legions could hold it. The undeniable fact was too the Empire as a military autocracy, subject to no constitutional law and liable to be the Emprie as a military autocarcy, subject to no constitutional law and liable to be transferred at any moment by military revolution. The merciful mask drawn over the ugly reality had its uses; the Empire could be made to look constitutional and, in seeming to be so, it might almost become so.

Of foreign policy the Emperor only talked to his clients now and then. Such high matters of state were usually reserved for him and his intimate advisers; the Senate was often called in to discuss, seldom to decide. Some events of interest and importance were deliberately brought to the public notice by coin-types. Such were the investiture of kings (*Rex Parthis Datus; Regna Adsignata; Rex Quadis Datus*) or the defeat and surrender of a province (*Iudaea Capta; Germania Capta; Dacia Capta*). It was the dazzling successes in particular that were advertised, successes that might seem to justify the vast labour and expense of wars. And still the triumph, now celebrated only by the Emperor or his sons, brought before the eyes of the Romans the detailed story of victory and conquest.

The Romans were acutely aware of the duality of life, of the material world, immediate, visible and tangible, and of the spirtiual world, remoter, out of sight or touch, but none the less real. His imagination roamed freely between the two. But we must not make the mistake of supposing that 'spiritual', in this context, implies anything vague or shadowy on the one hand or particularly good on the other. The supernatural was just the other side of the natural and, like it, contained elements of very diverse qualities. They were like the obverse and reverse of the same coin. As regards reality the spiritual world was more real than the material world, in the sense that in it the 'numina', the acts of divine will that make the world go round, have their being.

The Emperor, in his conversations with his clients, did not neglect this vital aspect of things. Of the forms of religion we have already had something to say; we must now speak about their content. It is mainly as the preservers of the Roman State and its Emperor that the gods are honoured. They can be cited as types of the Emperor in his various capacities. Jupiter represents him as lord and ruler, Mars as the warrior in arms, Hercules as the heroic toiler for mankind. Juno stands for the Empress, Minerva, vice-regent of Jupiter, for the prince. In this way, the activities of the great on earth could be set in a larger frame, be translated, so to speak, from time into eternity.

Only thus could the Roman world be felt to be firmly established. Zosimus, recording the sack of Rome by Alaric the Goth and the payment of his ransom, laments that the Romans were driven to melt down the images of those powers that had been honoured for their services in maintaining and prospering the Empire – among them that of the goddess whom the Romans called 'Virtus'. And then, he continues, all that was still left of courage and worth in Rome was quenched, as the masters of secret wisdom had long ago predicted. Virtus (equals Ῥώμη, Roma) must have been in a special sense the tutelary diety of the City. But all the gods have something of the same talismanic character. It is amazing to find that their images had survived in Rome so long into the Christian Empire.

Even more flexible and useful for propaganda was the world of the 'Virtues' – deities of the old Roman type, deities of pure function, without mythology, but capable of receiving worship. The *Virtus* exists, but where? Probably we should say in just those activities that make up her being. The Virtues might be appealed to in their general character, as *Pax, Felicitas, Concordia* or *Salus*. But they might also be associated with special occasions and persons, and, particularly in the latter case, the Virtue is felt to be a divine power, finding expression in the person through whom she acts. The Romans, before ever they built a temple to Julius Caesar himself, worshipped his Mercy (*Clementia*). The Emperor, by this worship of divine powers inherent in him, could be brought very near to the divine world. His character, policy and achievements could be expressed with much precision by the same device. For the Virtue of an Emperor is not just a quality of state of mind; it is an active power, a *numen*. Thus *Pax Augusti* is a definite power, which makes the Emperor a bringer of the Roman, the Augustan peace to the world. *Felicitas Augusti* certainly confers blessedness on the

Emperor himself, but she also flows out from him to make others blessed. *Sis felix nostrumque leves, quaecumque, laborem*, as Virgil in the *Aeneid* makes Aeneas say to his mother when she meets him disguised as a nymph.

The Virtues may be arranged in groups, covering the whole of life. War is under *Victoria* and *Honos* and *Virtus*, the patron deities of the army. Unless the Emperor is brave and valiant, he will not be Emperor for long. The Emperor Trajan, when he interrogated Ignatius and learned that he claimed to bear Christ in him, asked: 'And do you not believe that I have powers in me that give me victory over my enemies?' What he meant was *Victoria Augusti* and *Virtus Augusti*. *Pax* and *Felicitas* are concerned with peace and the prosperity that goes with it, and not far from them stand *Salus* and *Securitas*, salvation and peace of mind. Other Virtues are related to governmental departments – *Abundantia*, *Aequitas*, *Annona* and *Uberitas* to the Emperor's wealth of supply, *Moneta* to his mint. Others define the quality of an Emperor's government – *Clementia*, *Indulgentia*, *Iustitia*, *Libertas*, and *Tranquillitas*. *Liberalitas* and *Munificentia* inspire largesses and games, *Hilaritas* and *Laetitia* occasions of public rejoicing and merry-making. Fortune is the 'Luck of Empire.' *Genius* and *Bonus Eventus* both relate to the personality of the Emperor; occasionally, Juno, as feminine of Genius, is found for the Empress. *Concordia* is equally at home in the State and in the Imperial family; so, too, is *Pudicitia*, which can mean sacred purity as well as personal chastity. *Fides* is a virtue that pervades life, everywhere confirming and establishing the ties by which a social system is held together. The great religious Virtue is *Pietas*, 'Goodness', right conduct towards the gods or one's kindred or one's fellow men. *Pietas* to an enemy becomes almost our modern 'pity.'

The world of the Virtues was not closed, but could be expanded from time to time to meet new needs and express new desires. We have already spoken of the *Genius* or spirit of the Senate. Other *Genii* – of Roman people and army or of city – express the spiritual reality behind the material. The provinces, too, had their representations in human form; but though, like the gods and Virtues, they may bear distinguishing attributes, they probably did not normally receive cult and were not unlike our modern personifications – expressions of ideas in artistic and poetic form without much vitality. But the Virtues were alive, were powers like the Virtues in Milton's angelic orders, 'Thrones, Dominations, Princedoms, Virtues, Powers!' They were firmly conceived of; they had their distinguishing symbols. They were rooted in the soil of popular belief.

Finally, we may glance at a few wider conceptions, which might be built up out of a linked series of types and which an Emperor might wish to present emphatically to his subjects. One such conception is that of *Aeternitas*, the eternity of Rome, with which the eternity of the Imperial house is bound up, linked to the permanency of the natural order. Sun and moon are its natural symbols, or the phoenix, the bird reborn out of its own ashes. Present, past and future are bound together in an harmonious whole. But interest in the future was feeble compared with interest in the present and the past. There was no general ideal of progress: the Romans hardly had a word for the idea. The characteristic thought of the present is that of the ideal state, the *optimus status rerum*, ensured by an *optimus princeps*, endowed with the virtues necessary to produce it. Every reign that had time to define its programme tried to restate this theme of the *optimus status rerum* in new terms. But the present was firmly rooted in the past. The Romans had a deep respect for tradition, for the *mos maiorum*, and were not guilty of the modern heresy of imagining themselves 'self-made.' Right behind recorded history lay the Golden Age of myth – the Age of the old king Saturn in Latium or of the baby Jupiter in Crete – when Justice (*Astraea*) ruled the world, not yet driven away by men's sins, and the earth gave freely of her fruits to the holy race that reaped them. There was ever the dream, the hope that the ancient bliss could be restored, and Emperor after Emperor claims to be restoring that pristine virtue, happiness and plenty. Actually, you had to find your Golden Age in whatever the Emperor chanced to offer you. A Christian writer of the third century murmured in bitterness that the Golden Age was Iron in their experience. Still the theme persists; and, though definite reference to it, as on a well-known aureus of Hadrian, is very rare, it underlies the formula that so often occurs of *Felicitas saeculi, Felicitas temporum*. The *Fel. Temp. Reparatio*, the slogan of Constantius II and Constans for the eleven-hundredth year of Rome, moves in the same field of thought. Or, again, attention may be directed to the foundation of Rome, to Romulus the founder, or to the she-wolf and twins of legend; men may be invited to believe that Rome under its good Emperor is experiencing a new birth.

Here one must break off and cease to pursue a subject that seems to unfold itself unceasingly before us. I hope I have succeeded in convincing you that we can form some good general ideas of the imperial government and its subjects, and of the forms of thought that they shared in common, as also of the suggestions that were conveyed in those forms from governor to governed. The coins have been our chief guide; but their function is not only to deliver their own brief message, but to give us clues by which we may interpret much larger bodies of ancient evidence. I trust that our study has been of interest. I would plead that it is more than a curious piece of antiquarianism. It has a quite definite meaning for the present. In trying to realize the world of thought in which an ancient civilisation moved, we are led to compare it or contrast it with our own, and thus are enabled to realise with a new clearness what life means to a civilised society of today.*

* The ancient material, on which this paper draws, will be mainly found in the Catalogues of the coins of the Roman Empire in the British Musuem and the Bibliographies appended to them.

The Aristocratic Epoch in Latin Literature

R. E. SMITH

It is an honour not without responsibility to have been invited to deliver the first of these lectures in honour of the memory of the late Professor F. A. Todd. For Professor Todd was a Latin scholar of distinction, who was on the staff of the Department of Latin at this University for forty-one years, and for twenty-two of them until his death he guided the destinies of that Department. They were not easy years for those concerned for the future of classical studies: they called for resolution and sincerity of purpose, if in that changing world something was to be saved of the humanistic spirit in which he believed so deeply. Fortunately for this University those were Professor Todd's great qualities; qualities which showed in all his life, not least in his teaching and his scholarship. In neither would he surrender truth for the gaudy half-truth, hard work for leisured pseudo-learning; and we who follow after him must be grateful for the tradition thus created in the Department whose distinguished Head he was. And, therefore, while the honour done to me tonight is obvious, that honour imposes upon me a responsibility, that this, the foundation stone of the monument that is to do honour to his memory, shall be not unworthy of the man whose memory it will enshrine.

I have chosen for my subject tonight 'The Aristocratic Epoch in Latin Literature;' it is a subject of importance for an understanding of the growth and form of Latin literature, to which perhaps insufficient study has been given. But first I must make a few introductory remarks about the historical setting before proceeding to the subject proper.

The second century opened in Rome with the Hannibalic War brought to a successful conclusion and the Roman armies contending against Macedon; by the time of the Gracchi Rome had twice defeated and finally annexed Macedon, brought Antiochus the Great to heel, added to her responsibilities in Spain, Asia and Greece; had, in fact, assumed a considerable empire and no less considerable imperial responsibilities; in two generations she had become the greatest Mediterranean power, to whom all others deferred; whose every word throughout that world was law. The transition from an Italian to a Mediterranean power was necessarily attended with growing pains; but these in any normal growth may be expected, and had the growth been quite normal, Rome would have outgrown the pains to realize her potentialities. There were, however, attendant circumstances which made a simple process complex. Rome had come perforce into contact with the Greek world, a world that had much both good and bad to offer the less developed Rome; what she should absorb of this and what reject became one of the complicating factors. This alone would have taxed the wisdom of her governors, and it was not alone. The Hannibalic War had left large parts of Italy devastated; it and the wars that followed well nigh exhausted a treasury whose sources were designed to fill a humbler exchequer. The continued wars brought in their train the problem of finding soldiers; and this in its turn compelled the government to consider and reconsider its relations with the Latins and the Italians.

The yeoman farmer's fate, the basis of the state finances, Rome's relations with her allies, these were the problems that clamoured for solution to a government without experience in such novelties, and insufficiently aware of the nucleus of the problems for which she groped for answers. The influx of wealth from the East and the development of business and contracting which the constant wars made necessary, implied a development in the economy of Rome, and gave opportunities for the growth of a class whose wealth was not derived from the land. The transition from a purely agrarian economy to an economy that began to consist largely in taking what one wanted from other people was bound to have profound effects on the social structure of Rome; and this too, added to the complications of an already complex situation.

The nerve centre of the government in whose hands lay the fate of Rome was the Senate, and our period is known as that of Senatorial rule. It was under the Senate's guidance and direction that Rome had emerged triumphant from the Hannibalic War, and the prestige and experience which this body had gained during those years assured it a primacy in government that was not seriously challenged until 133 BC. In foreign affairs, in legislation and in the control – or lack of it – of the new economic influences the Senate's was the controlling voice. No one opposed its rulings, because on the whole its control seemed adequate and prudent; its success, the strength which came from its unrivalled experience, and the support which it enjoyed among the Italian nobility, would have condemned any challenge to failure.

The Senate consisted at this time of 300 members, but

the effective control of affairs was within the hands of a small group within this body, the *nobiles*. The old distinction between patrician and plebs had long ceased to have any importance; in its place had grown up a group of families whose ancestors had reached consular rank; the attainment of this office conferred nobility on the family, whose descendants were known as *nobiles*. Beneath them and less exclusive were the families who had attained praetorian rank. Access to the consulship was by now jealously guarded by the *nobiles*; for a *novus homo* to win his way to the office was exceedingly difficult, and, without the active support of some of the *nobiles*, impossible. How tight a hold they kept on the consulship the figures for these years show: during the 100 years preceding the tribunate of Tiberius Gracchus, out of 200 consulships 159 went to 26 families, 99 of them to only 10 families. Between 200 and 146 BC only 4 *novi homines* forced their way to the highest office, all of them helped by some section of the *nobiles*. The figures for the praetorship tell a not very different tale, though not within quite such narrow restrictions. Since the Senate was in its deliberations necessarily swayed by the advice and knowledge of those of its members whose experience in public affairs had been greatest, it followed that the effective power was in the hands of a few families, and that almost the only function of the humbler members was to support one or other of its leading personages.

Such in brief was the situation at Rome at the opening of the second century, such the instrument of government, and such the governors. When we survey Rome's literary achievements at this moment, we find little to inspire; Livius Andronicus had translated the Odyssey into Latin saturnians, and had translated and produced some Greek tragedies and comedies; Naevius had produced tragedies and comedies, based more or less on Greek models; he had introduced a new type of tragedy, the *praetexta*, which depended on Roman historical subjects for its plot; he had also completed the first Roman epic, the *Bellum Punicum*, written in saturnians; Ennius had been brought to Rome and had begun producing tragedies and comedies. Of literary prose there was nothing; Fabius Pictor's history of Rome, written in Greek, can hardly be counted as Latin literature. During the period with which we are concerned today, 200-133, will be found the great Roman dramatists, Ennius, Pacuvius, Caecilius, Plautus and Terence, Ennius's epic poem, the *Annales*, Lucilius the satirist, and the senatorial historians. There is little else of literature; and today I wish to enquire into this phenomenon, to see to what extent it was a result of the social life and the ideals of the community, and to what extent, if any, it was the result of limitations imposed by the attitude of the governing class. For, as we shall see, the social controls under the Senate were strict, and a closer inspection of the governing class may help us to an understanding of this problem.

On reading one of Plutarch's lives of late third century or second century Romans, we must be struck by its difference not merely from a comparable Greek life but even from a later Roman life. Whereas in the latter we have personal anecdotes, not infrequently scandalous stories, schemes of motivation based on Plutarch's interpretation of the character, which he inferred from numerous anecdotes and sayings attributed to the subject, in the former we are confronted with a certain statuesqueness. The narrative is confined almost wholly to the character's public life; there is something of his family, little of his education, seldom an enlightening anecdote; and even in the public life Plutarch hardly ventures beyond the strictly formal narrative of history. For motivation we look almost in vain; Plutarch does his best to explain the character's behaviour; but his explanation seldom goes beyond some abstract idea such as φιλοτιμία, which has to work in a vacuum for lack of true material. We are given an explanation of Fabius's opposition to Scipio's plans for transferring the war to Africa, namely his personal opposition to Scipio and his general policy. But this is exceptional, though the history of these years must have contained many examples of such conflicts between the leading men, whose personal policies were the basis of the Roman policy.

The absence of these elements from the Lives is strange, since we know that elsewhere Plutarch introduces them, and they are in Plutarch's estimation important for an understanding of the character; we can, therefore, only infer that they are missing from these Lives because Plutarch could nowhere light upon the necessary material. If we can discover why such material was not available, we shall go a long way to understanding the attitude and outlook of those who made the history of these years, dictated the social policy, and kept a watchful eye on those who were making a Latin literature. For the sources for such information would have been the contemporary literature of various kinds similar to that upon which he drew for his other Lives.

We must return to the *nobiles*, and ask ourselves whether we can discover their ideals at this time. We are helped in this enquiry by the fact that at Rome the family was a closely knit organization. The family claimed a man's first loyalty, and its different members were bound together by the common religion of the *gens*. The practice of lining the walls of the *atrium* with the *imagines* of the ancestors, with their achievements outlined in the *tituli* beneath them, contributed to breed a pride in the family, which would be encouraged by the contents of the family archives, wherein would be found *laudationes*, the magisterial notes of holders of office and similar material. This family pride, by no means unjustifiable, had developed by this time until it almost weighed upon the young member of an outstanding family. Polybius has a charming story of the young Scipio Aemilianus's confession of his uneasiness on this score.[1] The two were one day walking along together, when the young Scipio suddenly addressed him as follows: 'Why is it, Polybius, that though I and my brother eat at the same table, you address all your conversation to him, and pass me over altogether? Of course you too have the same opinion of me as I hear the rest of the city has. For I am considered by everyone, I hear, to be a mild effete person, and far removed from the true Roman character and ways, because I don't care for pleading in the law courts. And they say the family I come of requires a different kind of representative, and not the sort a that I am. That is what annoys me most.'

At the funeral of these great men a speech, called a *laudatio*, was spoken to the crowd; in it were outlined the outstanding achievements and virtues of the dead man and of his ancestors; men dressed up and wearing the masks of his ancestors took part in the funeral procession. On the tombs were cut *elogia*, short commemorative verses, outlining the public offices and activities of the dead man. We are fortunate in possessing some of the *elogia* from the tomb of the Scipios, as well as an extract from a *laudatio* pronounced in honour of the Metellus who died in 221 BC. We will glance at these to see if perhaps we may distil from them the aristocrats' conception of *virtus*.

The earliest of the *elogia* is that in memory of Lucius Scipio, son of Scipio Barbatus, and reads as follows: 'Here lies a man amongst good men the very best, most Romans do agree, Lucius Scipio, Barbatus' son. Consul, censor, aedile was he amongst you. Corsica and Aleria did he take in battle; to the Weather gods gave he in thank-offering a temple he had vowed.'[2] It confines itself to the public life, and after listing his offices refers to his most distinguished service to the State and to the gods. The next one, on his father, follows similar lines: 'Cornelius Lucius Scipio Barbatus, son of Gnaeus, brave man and wise, whose handsome looks his virtue did quite match; consul, censor, aedile was he amongst you; Taurasium, Cisaunum he captured in Samnium; all Lucania did he o'erwhelm and hostages take off.'[3] There is here a greater flexibility of expression; otherwise the two are parallel. The next two belong to a later period, when the Hellenic influence was well-established at Rome; they are both in honour of men who died young, before they could have held major office or excelled in public life; the first one runs thus: 'Death brought to pass that all things thine were short, honours, fame, virtue, glory, and talents. Had it been vouchsafed to thee in a long life to make the most of these, featly thy ancestors' feats hadst thou surpassed. Wherefore with goodwill into her bosom, Scipio, doth Earth receive thee, Publius Cornelius called, Publius thy sire.'[4] No one can miss the Hellenic influence, but it is confined to externals, turns of phrase and neatness of expression. The saturnian metre is still employed, in spite of Ennius, and more particularly, the concept of what constituted a good and successful life remains the same. 'Honours, fame, virtue, glory and talents' still as a hundred years earlier are the elements of a successful life, and continue so in the next *elogium*, also in honour of a young man: 'Great wisdom and many virtues in a short life this tomb contains; life, not honour, deserted the honours of him who is laid here, a man never surpassed in virtue. At twenty years he was laid here to rest; seek not his honours, he was not entrusted with any.'[5] We see the constancy of the ideal, consisting still in public honours and public office, to the extent that even where the dead man took no part in public life, the only comment is on what he would have done had he lived longer. In the last one elegiac metre has at last ousted the saturnian metre. It is preceded by a list of his public offices and then continues: 'I added to the virtues of my family by my character, I had children, and sought to equal my father's deeds. I won the praise of my ancestors, so that they are glad that I was one of them; my honours ennobled my stock.'[6]

We notice at once throughout all these *elogia* the exclusive concern with public life and office and distinction won in the public service: *fortis, sapiens, honor, fama, virtus, ingenium*, these represent the desirable qualities in their estimation. There is an almost regal tone about the two earliest 'I was your consul.' In the latest there is perhaps a suggestion of family self-consciousness, which was absent from the earlier ones; their families' pre-eminence was taken for granted. It is a sign that the aristocracy were becoming self-consciously aristocratic, because of attacks on their previously accepted pre-eminence. By this time Cato had been drawing attention to some of their weaknesses; and perhaps more important, the nobles had been subjected to bitter criticism as a result of their earlier incompetence in Spain.

We may now turn to the extract from the *laudatio* of Metellus; after cataloguing all his public offices, it continues:[7] 'Metellus wished to be a champion warrior, the best orator, the bravest general, to hold command in the greatest undertakings, to meet with highest official preferment, to be a leader in wisdom, to be deemed the leading Senator, to gain great wealth by honest means, to leave many children, and to be the most distinguished man of the state. These things fell to his lot, and to the lot of no other man since the founding of Rome.' There is the aristocrat's ideal plain for all to see, to be a leading man in the State's service both in war and in peace. To leave many children is an ideal common to many aristocracies, who fear lest the family may die out. The adoption of children by leading families in our period is a testimony to the liveliness of this sentiment. Two sons of Aemilius Paullus were adopted into great houses: one to become Scipio Aemilianus, the other to become a Fabius. We note also that the possession of wealth was among their ideals and this, too, need not surprise us; a line of Ennius that speaks of 'a man of no great substance, yet full trustworthy' illustrates this aspect of the ideal in its assumption that normally a man of no great substance would not be trustworthy.

This aristocratic ideal is to be found embedded even in the fragments of Ennius; such lines as '*qualis consiliis quantumque potesset in armis*,'[8] '*quem nemo ferro potuit superare nec auro*.'[9] '*fortes Romani sunt tamquam caelus profundus*,'[10] or '*moribus antiquis stat res Romana virisque*,'[11] all alike breathe the same ideal, the same high purpose of public service. At the end of our period, when corruption had set in amongst certain of their class, it was against betrayals of this ideal that Lucilius inveighed. For an ideal of public service carries with it a sense of responsibility in the execution of that work; if a class marks itself off as a governing class, then its whole behaviour must be worthy of such a claim; and it was against lapses from this implied code of behaviour, whether in private or in public life, that Lucilius's attacks were directed. Lucilius's own definition of *virtus* states the same ideals, to which the Scipionic circle is vainly trying to recall the weaker nobles. The *elogia*, the fragments of Ennius and of Lucilius all in their different ways presuppose and illustrate this ideal of public service; the *elogia* in the simple pride of a life of distinguished public service; Ennius in making it the mainspring of his characters' actions, the explanation of Rome's greatness;

Lucilius by his criticism of those who had fallen from it, and the implication of its existence as the norm by which he judges his victims.

I call this the aristocratic ideal; others, no doubt, would accept it and maybe try to live up to it in their humbler way; but the pattern was made by the nobles, whose opportunities for public service were so much greater than others'. And ordinary men and women were not constantly aware either of their proud ancestry, because they had none, or of their public service, because their lives were not governed by such considerations. A sepulchral inscription, somewhat later in time, of a youth who died at the age of twenty may serve by contrast with the Scipionic *elogium* on the twenty-year-old to show the cleavage between the nobles and those with no *stemmata* and no ambitions in public life: 'Gnaeus Taracius, son of Gnaeus, lived twenty years. His bones are laid here. Alas, alas! Taracius, how bitter the fate to which you were delivered! The years of your life were not all spent when you were given up to death; but at the time when it behoved you to be living in the flower of the age of youth, you passed away and left your mother in grief and sorrow.'[12] Here is a perfectly simple epitaph, expressing personal sorrow in simple terms, with no thought of family pride or of public service. We must remember that most men and women at Rome were like this woman; they acknowledged and respected 'the quality,' allowed their superiority and without demur handed over to them the complicated task of government, expecting in return only such tokens of recognition at election and other times as had become by now almost traditional.

This office-holding nobility, supported in its ideals by the lesser members of the Senate, took a lofty view of its responsibilities in the maintenance of the tone, or *ethos*, of the Roman State; necessarily, because as they identified themselves with the State, whose governance they had made so peculiarly their own, the State must confrom to their own ideal; their conception of *virtus*, embodied in their own lives, must be reflected in the general tone of the object of their care. Our period saw the great inrush of Hellenic influence in the form of literature, philosophy, art, and by no means least the Greeks themselves. Such influences were in no way new to Rome; Etruria had profoundly influenced Rome in art, architecture and religion since the time of the kings; and though the influence of Etruria was no longer felt at Rome, she had learnt from this experience how to adopt and to adapt. More important for our purpose was the influence of Magna Graecia; this influence had been at first indirect, by way of Etruria and Southern Latium; but since the Pyrrhic War and the capture of Tarentum Rome had come into direct contact with the highly developed Greek culture of Southern Italy, and from this contact had already learnt and absorbed much. We may regard as a symbol of this new, direct influence the bringing to Rome, as a slave, of Livius Andronicus, captured at Tarentum, who became the father of Latin literature and the first teacher at Rome. During the Punic War Sicily had been one of the important theatres of combat; there the Roman army had been brought into close contact with a flourishing Greek civilization, and at Syracuse with a city which had attained a high level of culture, and whose buildings and private houses were of a beauty and luxury quite unknown at Rome. The story of Marcellus's sack of Syracuse need not be repeated here; sufficient to recall the plundering of public and private buildings, the vast booty shipped to Rome, consisting of works of art of all kinds, to show that the work of the Greek artistic genius was not unknown to Rome by 200 BC.

When, therefore, the Romans first came into direct

contact with Greece itself, they were not ignorant barbarians, tasting for the first time a higher and more artistic civilization; the Philhellenism of Scipio or Flamininus in 200 BC would in that case be inexplicable; it was this earlier acquaintance with an art and literature to which Rome had no counterpart that aroused among the better minds an appreciation for these things and made them ready to steep themselves more deeply in them should opportunity offer. They approached Greece as Philhellenes; their contact with Greece served only to modify and moderate their earlier enthusiasms.

The fruits of this contact between Rome and Greece after 200 BC I am not here concerned to describe; the Hellenic influence on art and literature and on the social life of Rome is known to most persons in general terms at least. But it is easy to form an exaggerated idea of its effects; to see it in its true perspective is less easy. The aspects to which I wish to draw attention today is the limit of their absorption, from which we may be able to discover the reasons why the boundary mark was set in one place and not in another. I will begin by taking two examples from the realm of religion.

In the year 205 BC a fresh outburst of *religio* on the part of the people demanded some fresh action from the government. The people had been prone to these outbursts throughout the Hannibalic War, and the government had been compelled to resort to all sorts of religious contrivances in an effort to allay the panic. On this occasion they made their usual approach to the Sibylline books, and returned with the inspired answer that any foreign foe that had invaded Italy would be driven out and defeated if the Romans brought to Rome the Idaean Mother from Pessinus. This was a clear attempt to allay the present panic by the introduction of a novelty, since the old cures had begun to be less effective. Both Delphi and

Scipio himself supported this idea, and a suitably appointed embassy was sent to King Attalus, through whose good offices they hoped to become possessed of the goddess. The envoys called at Delphi on the way, were encouraged and told to see that the best man at Rome welcomed her on arrival. The Senate decided that P. Scipio was the 'best of good men' at Rome, and he accordingly went to meet the ship at Ostia, together with the leading matrons, whose duty it was to accompany the goddess on the journey from Ostia to Rome. The 'goddess' consisted of a black meteoric stone, who was duly received by Scipio and escorted to Rome by the matrons, who took turns to carry her, while the people burned incense at their doors as the procession passed.

Thus the Magna Mater came to Rome, to stay a passing panic. But very soon the Senate discovered that orgiastic rites were connected with her worship, and their reaction was quick and firm: it was ordained by a *senatus consultum* that no Roman should take part in her service. The inference is clear; they had been quite ready to humour the people by the introduction of a fresh goddess, while they thought that her presence would not affect the Roman *ethos*; but as soon as the unpleasant truth was realized that connected with her worship were rites that conflicted with the *mos maiorum*, they at once sought to prevent its evil effects by banning the orgiastic ritual to Romans.

My second case may be dealt with more briefly. In 186 BC the Senate discovered that the worship of Dionysus had reached disquieting proportions throughout Italy; that in the course of this worship secret societies were formed, orgiastic ritual indulged in and strange oaths taken. The Senate acted with a firmness that may surprise our modern tolerance; regarding it as subversive activity, and considering such activity in social matters to be no less dangerous than in political, by a legal fiction it pronounced the whole affair *coniuratio*, rebellion, in this case against the established ways of Rome, the *mos maiorum*. With the help of the allies the worship was suppressed, though those who sincerely wished to continue in the practice were allowed to do so, provided that not more than six persons collected in any one group.

Again we see the Senate prepared to make concessions to the people, provided only that Rome remained Roman, that the Roman *ethos* was not destroyed. When we reflect on the increasing number of foreign slaves and South Italians who were finding their way to Rome, and the manifold influences which were conspiring to change or upset the Roman and Italian outlook after the turmoil of war, the contacts during service with other ways of life, especially in the East, the economic and social changes already in process, we can perceive that the government was dealing with a twofold problem of absorption, one of people and one of ideas.

The realm of philosophy shows the Senate applying similar limitations. The better Romans were attracted to Greek philosophy, and not seldom visited Athens to meet the leading philosophers; a visit to Athens began to form part of the education of the young noble. Titus Flamininus had spent time at Athens; Aemilius Paullus had the library of King Perseus brought to Rome for the use of his growing sons. It might have seemed in such an atmosphere that Greek philosophers would be welcome visitors to Rome. Yet we are at first sight perplexed at the apparently inconsistent behaviour of the Senate; at one moment they seem friendly, at the next they appear to be narrowly prejudiced against those very people at whose feet their sons would gladly sit in Athens or elsewhere. In the year 161 BC philosophers and *rhetores* were banished from Rome; in 154 BC Diogenes, Critolaus and Carneades, who were representing Athens as ambassadors to Rome, were hustled untimely out of Rome, their business having been rushed through the Senate at Cato's instigation. Yet at this same time Polybius was living with Scipio, and about ten years later Panaetius, the distinguished Stoic, was to spend two years with Scipio, without protest from anyone.

This might seem strange at first; but let us look briefly at Plutarch's description of the second incident, the riddance of the embassy.[13] 'The charm,' he says, 'of Carneades especially, which had boundless power, and a fame not inferior to its power, won large and sympathetic audiences and filled the city, like a rushing mighty wind, with the sound of his praises. Report spread far and wide that a Greek of amazing talent, who disarmed all opposition by the magic of his eloquence, had infused a tremendous passion into the youth of the city, in consequence of which they forsook their other pleasures and pursuits and were "possessed" of philosophy. . . . Cato, at the very outset, when this zeal for discussion came pouring into the city, was distressed, fearing lest the young men, by giving this direction to their ambition, should come to love a reputation based on mere words more than one achieved by martial deeds. And when the fame of the philosophers rose yet higher in the city . . . Cato determined on some pretext or other to rid and purge the city of them all. So he rose in the Senate . . . and said: 'We ought to make up our minds one way or another . . . in order that these men may return to their schools and lecture to the sons of Greece, while the youth of Rome give ear to their laws and magistrates, as heretofore.'

The fact that this suggestion was complied with shows that Cato was not alone in his uneasiness. The last sentence gives the clue to Cato's and the Senate's uneasy feelings; they wanted the youth of Rome to continue to obey the laws and the magistrates. Obedience to the constituted authority, *disciplina*, was the foundation of the Roman State; their early history was filled with improving stories in illustration of this virtue; the greatness of the Roman army depended upon this absolute obedience to higher authority, and disobedience was sternly punished. It was safe enough for the nobles themselves to learn the art of thinking and questioning accepted views, and this they had done and were to continue to do, for they could on the whole trust themselves to pay the deference to one another which was required of a private citizen to a magistrate; and since they were the class from whom the senior magistrates came, loyalty to their class was a sufficient safeguard. But these philosophers and rhetoricians had at Rome not confined themselves to the nobles; they had been giving lectures to which anyone could listen, and the result had been that the young men were beginning to question the traditional conceptions of duty, right and wrong. This appeared to strike at the very root of the Roman *ethos*, and further, at the root of the power of the *nobiles*, for by now the two had become interdependent, each deriving part of its strength from the other. The very cleverness of Carneades was his undoing and the nobles' reaction was to remove these disturbing elements from the people's midst.

But if we can understand in what these philosophers sinned, can we appreciate why Polybius and Panaetius were so welcome? The answer is that in both cases they interpreted history and philosophy in terms agreeable to the Roman *ethos*. Polybius's history was an interpretation of Roman history according to the aristocratic ideal, for which he had a profound admiration. Even when it became clear to him that the ideal state was ceasing to be, he failed to discern the social and economic causes that were ending the nobles' régime through their failure resolutely to grapple with them, and found it in the falling away of individual nobles from their own ideal. The qualities he singles out in his character sketches are just those which the aristocratic ideal valued most highly: scrupulous honesty, comparative poverty in spite of opportunity for acquiring wealth; duty to the family and so forth.[14] And it is the lack of such qualities which he notes as characteristic of some of the nobles in the latter part of our period, the time when he had seen the first signs of the breakdown of his ideal form of government. His whole interpretation of Roman history presupposes the existence of a dominant nobility, and the praise which he bestows on them both as a class and individually is a testimony to his approval of their existence and their behaviour.

The case of Panaetius was very similar. To this great philosopher Rome was indebted for the philosophical interpretation of her character and her aims. He made possible the humanization of Roman law, to become the first legal system to embrace within its comprehensive conception the whole human race. Yet his immediate success and subsequent influence were due to his sympathetic approach to the Roman mind and character. Equipped with the intellectual arms of Greece, endued with the panoply of Stoicism, he might have found a welcome no warmer than did Carneades. But in his way he was a greater man; by his sympathetic understanding of the Roman character and their ideals he was able to win the confidence of the Romans. He did not seek to dazzle by the brilliance of his logic; he was content to adapt his Stoicism to Roman needs. He took the Roman *ethos* and the aristocratic ideal and gave them a philosophical basis; Stoicism and the ideal became fused in his interpretation. Nothing of the essential elements was changed, nothing was added; the ideal and the *ethos* remained as before, but now they seemed to have a basis in the order of the world, whereas before their only appeal had been to tradition and *mos maiorum*.

Poseidonius in the first century continued in this tradition, and it is interesting to observe the degree to which Stoicism and the ideal had become one. Tiberius Gracchus was supposed to have been advised and encouraged in his plans for reform by Blossius, a Stoic, though not, it seems, in the tradition of Panaetius. The aims of the Gracchi must, it would have seemed, have commended themselves to a Stoic. Yet Poseidonius in his history of Rome adopted a hostile attitude towards the Gracchi, and his criticisms make clear the reason for this hostility: their precipitate action had brought into jeopardy the established government of the nobles, and had begun the movement which was to lead through demagogues and dictators to Empire. When Poseidonius wrote, the movement was under way, and though he might not foresee the end he could see the irreparable damage done to the aristocratic ideal.

Such was the attitude of the Roman nobility towards religion and philosophy, based as we have seen on their position as the effective governors of the State, to whose continuance as a Roman state, in the narrow sense in which they interpreted that conception, their energies and power were directed. Having noted the manner in which they sought to control undesirable intrusions into the realm of religious and philosophic beliefs, we may now turn to examine their attitude to literature, to see if a similar censorship was maintained in the sphere of letters, and if so, how and to what degree it influenced the course of Latin letters. We must deal separately with prose and poetry, since owing to the different content of the two forms the nobles adopted correspondingly different attitudes.

We will deal first with poetry. We have seen that their ideal was one of public service; such an ideal left little opportunity for the professional poet, and in earlier times little chance to appreciate a poet's works. 'Men used not to respect the poet's art; anyone that gave his attention to it or spent his time at parties was called a 'vagabond.' Thus wrote Cato[15] in the first half of the second century, and the time to which he is referring is not a misty past but a comparatively recent one. The poet and the parasite at that time were equally the object of scorn and contempt. That attitude had changed; under the influence of Hellenism they had come to appreciate poetry, but they themselves took no active part in it. True, we find during our period aristocrats composing poems, such as Mummius, brother of the man who sacked Corinth; but they were not to be taken seriously. They were merely a sign of an educated man, one of his accomplishments. Suetonius tells us[16] that as a result of Crates's visit to Rome in 159 BC men dug out from their obscurity old poems of their own or their friends, carefully revised them and read them before circles of friends for criticism and comment. The story is in itself sufficient to give us the picture of the amateur poets of the time, regarding verse-making as an educated refinement, at which it behoved the cultured man to try his hand. Suetonius tells us that apart from Scipio Aemilianus and Laelius, Q. Fabius Labeo, C. Sulpicius Galba and M. Popilius were all persons who might have helped Terence in writing his plays. This statement reveals two facts: first, that some aristocrats were thought to be able poets; second, that though they were, it would have been unbecoming in them to produce plays under their own name, and that they would therefore have cloaked their Muse under the name of Terence.

But if such was their attitude towards the profession of poet in their own persons, they did not necessarily despise the poet as such, nor condemn his works. Livius had been the first Roman poet: he had translated the *Odyssey* into saturnians; and had thus produced a national Italian epic. For the story of Odysseus and his wanderings had far closer association with Italy than with Greece, and Odysseus was something, therefore, of an Italian hero. Naevius and Ennius had gone further and produced instead of Italian Roman epics. All three had helped to bring their readers to a consciousness of their country, the latter two of their destiny and their inherent greatness. Livius also produced plays for the Roman stage; at this time the connexion between religion and the stage was close, and the production of plays was a contribution towards the changing ritual of Roman religion. He was called upon in the critical later stage of the Hannibalic War to write a religious hymn, and in token of his services to the State was founded what was later known as the Collegium Poetarum on the Aventine. We may see how the nobility were not slow to reward the ex-slave for his service to the State.

Naevius, too, wrote for the Roman stage; and in comedy the example of the old Attic comedy was to hand, with all its free criticism of leading personalities and of politics; and the Latin spirit was by no means opposed to this freedom. It was not therefore surprising that this freedom of speech and criticism should be imitated at Rome, and in fact it was, by Naevius. We are told that he criticized leading men, and we still possess a fragment[17] in which the youthful follies of the great Scipio are retailed: it runs as follows:

> Even him whose hand did oft
> Accomplish mighty exploits gloriously,
> Whose deeds wane not, but live on to this day,
> The one outstanding man in all the world,
> Him, with a single mantle, his own father
> Dragged from a lady-love's arms.[18]

We are further told that because of his boldness Naevius

was imprisoned, and was released through the intervention of a tribune, and that after giving further offence of a like kind he was finally banished. That was the beginning and the end of the spirit of old comedy on the Roman stage in our period, and we may pause a moment here to note the significance of Naevius's treatment.

The stage was the one means of communicating, so to speak, with the Roman people at large. The reading public was a very small one, confined naturally to the educated classes; and these were chiefly the governing classes. In these circumstances censorship of literature was not felt to be necessary. But persistent criticism of the nobles and their policy from the stage could only end in cheapening them in the eyes of the people, and was likely to lead eventually to a lack of obedience towards the constituted authorities. Its first manifestation was therefore silenced, and the successors of Naevius were too wise to attempt its resuscitation. At the end of our period we come upon direct criticism of the nobles in the satires of Lucilius, but we must not lightly conclude that they therefore allowed unbridled criticism. Lucilius's satires were for a reading public, and further were written under the aegis of the leading statesman of the day, Scipio Aemilianus. Their first audience was the Scipionic circle, their second the nobles whom he castigated; at no time was there any danger that the weaknesses of the nobles would become reading matter for the general public; indeed, it is probably true that Scipio himself, a great upholder of the aristocratic tradition, encouraged him to his work, for the express object of recalling the peccant nobles to a sense of their duties and responsibilities as members of the governing class.

It is not surprising therefore that Plautus preferred to restrict his activities to the *fabula palliata*. And even within this sphere he knew what the nobles wanted and what would give displeasure. He was too wise to make Rome the scene of any of his plays. Not merely does he adapt Greek plays, but he is most careful to keep the whole colouring Greek, to leave no doubt that what he is depicting on the stage could not have happened at Rome. The impudent slaves, the dishonest sons, could be laughed at by the Roman audience because they were completely foreign to Rome, and therefore the morals of Rome were not impugned. It would never have done to suggest that the Roman *paterfamilias* was outwitted by his son, or that slaves were for ever scoring off their masters. When comedies in Roman settings began to be written, Donatus tell us[19] that the role of the slave had to be toned down, because Roman sentiment would not have tolerated a master being outwitted by his slave. For similar reasons Plautus had to tread carefully in his portrayal of female character; the *hetaera* could not be shown on the Roman stage as a generous character, since the Roman matrons would have objected; he was therefore compelled to make her an inferior character with little to commend her. In his whole approach we find Plautus accepting the limitations which the governing class insisted on imposing on all aspects of public life. Within those limitations he could and did work freely; as a professional playwright he could not afford to run counter to the sentiments of the governing class, and his genius succeeded in producing plays which both pleased his audience and satisfied the conditions imposed.

Titinius first attempted to bring the scene to Italy, though not to Rome; he wrote *fabulae togatae*, in which he laid the scenes in small Italian townships. It is perhaps not unimportant to note that he did not make Rome the scene; Mommsen supposed that the author of *togatae* was obliged to confine his activities to cities with Latin rights, and that the presentation of Rome or cities with full citizenship was forbidden. The result was that as the citizenship gradually expanded so did the area in which a scene might be laid contract. Whether it was expressly forbidden we cannot say, nor does it matter; it is sufficient that we realize that such was the position, and we need not be surprised that it was so. A class that was so concerned for the maintenance of the Roman *ethos* was unlikely to look with equanimity at plays whose plot revolved around the loose morals of Roman citizens, or in which slaves were called upon to help their masters' sons in some deception at the expense of the *paterfamilias*. And even in the atmosphere of the small Italian towns care must needs be exercised, since Rome depended on their friendship and support, and their ruling classes seem to have been in close alliance with the Roman nobles. Unfortunately we have none of Titinius's plays, but it seems that he paid particular attention to his female characters who would presumbably take the place of the Greek *hetaera* for which the Roman stage had no place. He further, we are told, toned down the impudence of the slave, and we may be tolerably certain that sons were not so able at deceiving their fathers.

With Terence we need not concern oursleves at length. He enjoyed the patronage of Scipio, who took a lively interest in his work. With Terence we begin to feel that the literary quality of the play is the author's first considera-tion; the humanism which infuses all his work reveals a sensitive nature which had no wish to compete with tight rope walkers, even if it could. But the fact that the Roman public's taste was becoming cruder just when the leading aristocrat was interesting hinself in the work of Rome's leading playwright suggests a certain artificiality in the play *qua* play. Its first object was to be a good play judged by literary standards, and its spirit was to be that of the humanism of the Scipionic circle. But there was not and could not be any question of conflict between the playwright and the government; they were now in open alliance.

It is not perhaps mere accident that nearly all the dramatists were non-Romans by birth, and some of them ex-slaves. The fact that most of them depended on their success as playwrights or on patronage to eke out an existence gave the governing class a hold on their work, which they did not hesitate to exercise. The Romans themselves were unable to write plays at this time; the educated class turned deliberately away from the practice of letters, while the rest of Rome lived in an atmosphere of practical life which did not encourage the native genius to find expression in literature. Personal poetry does not flourish in a closely-welded society; there must be an atmosphere of individualism, even if it is in resistance to social restraints, before there can be individual expression; and at Rome in the second century there was not that atmosphere. A foreigner may write a play for others; he cannot express their inmost thoughts for them. Epic there might have been, but for that, too, the atmosphere was no longer suitable. The defeat of Carthage had impressed the Romans no less than the rest of the world; they had felt they were called to some destiny on this earth. Naevius and Ennius had given expression to that feeling, and helped the Romans to perceive their destiny. But that feeling had gone; true, the better Romans were still conscious of a responsibility and a destiny; but things went too well; without the death struggle against Hannibal to sustain them and make them feel their purpose, how could they be filled with a sense of destiny? Their only concern was with the routine of office and empire. Not until a century of upheaval and civil war had made them feel their failure, could another epic interpret Rome's high destiny, when after the stormy passage they seemed to be in port, and they needed encouragement to put to sea once more.

Such other poetry as the nobles did encourage was in their own praise. The story of how Fulvius Nobilior took Ennius with him to Ambracia in order that he might write up his accomplishments is known to all. Scipio, too, used Ennius to sing his praises; and Accius composed some verses in honour of Brutus Gallaecus, which were inscribed on a temple he had erected. The form of tragedy, *fabula praetexta*, which dealt with Roman themes of history, served its purpose too; there was no mockery or criticism; the central figure was a hero, held up for the edification of the people, while the part of Roman history with which it dealt was depicted in such a way as to evoke the pride of the people who had helped to make it; and this would contribute towards an approval of the aristocratic policy that lay behind it. Thus and thus only might Rome and Romans appear upon the stage.

The nobles' attitude to poetry is thus clear: they would not give their own efforts to it, though they allowed others to, provided what they wrote supported or at least did not conflict with the *ethos* of Rome as they interpreted it. The *mos maiorum*, the Roman character and the underlying assumptions concerning the organization of the State and the duties of the different classes within it were alike topics about which there was no compromise; support or silence was the only choice open to the poet; and it followed that the leading personalities of the State were sacrosanct.

But with prose the case was different. Latin prose was not at the beginning of our period the flexible instrument for communicating the whole gamut of human thought and emotions that it later became under Cicero's influence. It was stiff, unyielding, and was used chiefly for purposes of business, the chronicling of laws, of treaties, and all the purposes of State; there was a nascent oratory, hardly less stiff and unadorned. Men did not yet turn to this medium in which to express any but the most concrete of sentiments. One form of prose composition did, however, develop during this period, that of historical composition. Rome, when she was engaged with Hannibal, felt the need to make her motives known to the world of Greece; and when that war was over, the need became even greater. Once they were inextricably involved with that world, whose culture and civilization they admitted to be superior to their own, and of whose goodwill they stood in need, the necessity to show the purity of their motives to nations brought up to believe only in wiles and tricks became even more pressing; especially when they wanted to be friendly – on their own terms, we agree – with parts at any rate of the Greek world. The Greeks were scornful of barbarians and lesser breeds; and those Greeks that had taken the trouble to try to understand Rome's motives had formed an adverse opinion of her intentions. The interpretation of Roman institutions in Rome and confederate institutions in Italy must therefore come from Rome; and since the aims and policy which required interpretation and explanation to the Greeks were those of the nobles, who fashioned Roman policy, it was natural that the interpretation, too, should come from them. They alone had the secret, and the wish, and hence arose that group of Senatorial historians who described for the Greek world in the Greek tongue Roman and Italian institutions and the Senatorial policy. The same intention lay behind the letters which we know Scipio Africanus and later Scipio Nasica wrote to foreign kings, describing in detail recent Roman campaigns.

It is true that family ambition found an outlet in these histories, and that the authors did not scruple to exaggerate the achievements of their ancestors, perhaps at the expense of other families. But that is not to say either that they criticized other families, or that what they wrote was read by the ordinary Roman citizen, and hence any criticism implicit or explicit was not dangerous. Further, these historians restricted themselves to public life; their accounts were not embellished by sordid or fanciful stories of private life in the manner of some of the Greek historians; any distortion there might have been did not extend beyond the military or public achievements of rivals. Thus arose the one branch of letters to which the educated class gave their time during our period, and that not primarily from a love of letters but for the strictly practical purpose of explaining their own motives to a foreign world.

When the elder Cato took up his pen to compose his *Origines*, the first to use the Latin tongue for Roman history, he, too, had a clear objective, to make the Italian cities conscious of their common destiny with Rome. His whole political career was one of opposition to the leading nobles; a *novus homo*, who affected to despise the Hellenic culture, he represented to a marked degree the Italian element in Roman politics, and thus of necessity found himself in opposition to those who laid great store by Hellenism. The first of his family to attain high office, he had no patience with those who claimed such office as a birthright, men whose concern for the honour of their family was such that in their histories they even falsified the true account. These considerations shaped the form and content of the *Origines*; the essential unity of Italy and of Italian and Roman history was made apparent by the scheme of the work; and his refusal to name commanders other than by their rank, while at the same time naming a military tribune or an elephant which had earned distinction by some act of bravery, was a direct snub to the Senatorial historians who had been only too ready to parade the names of their illustrious family members. But it, too, was not intended for the ordinary

Roman public; its readers were the educated classes in the Italian cities, the governing classes in their communities, whose co-operation and support Cato saw clearly were essential for the orderly progress of Rome.

Of oratory we need make here no mention; it grew out of the needs of State, out of the need for a man to persuade his fellows, to convince his opponents, or to express his country's policy before the ambassadors of other countries. Its first purpose was to be spoken, not written; and although speeches were undoubtedly committed to writing during our period, the main purpose of this practice was that there might be an enduring record of the policies and opinions expressed. We are confronted therefore once more with motives similar to those which prompted the writing of history; and if the Roman people did not read the one, it is quite certain they would not read the other. Publication of these speeches would serve their more immediate political purposes in two ways: first by providing a permanent record of their policy; and secondly – and here we are particularly concerned with speeches made in political prosecutions and defences – by committing to permanent record their attacks on their opponents. This second purpose, of course, equally subserved political ends, and this was probably the first consideration in publishing them; and though the speeches may have had literary qualities, it was not those qualities which induced their publication.

There was during our period no other prose worthy of the name; such as there was had a utilitarian object, and was designed for the small educated public of the time. We can now see therefore the extent to which the aristocracy dominated the literary scene of their day. Cultured as they were, their upbringing and traditions designed them for men of action in the State; this was their first concern and on this their ambitions centred. The life of contemplation and literature was for them a pastime or a means of relaxation; in no circumstances was it their main goal. The consequence was that though they might and did encourage poets, yet poetry was bound to depend on men from outside for its expression, since the one class with sufficient education at Rome deliberately restricted its exercise to the fireside. And the limits within which Roman poetry might be written by non-Romans were fairly narrow, and were confined to dramatic poetry, which, since it was not strictly a native product and depended largely on Greek influence for its inspiration, was the preserve of any person with a knowledge of the Latin tongue. And even in this sphere the nobles' concern for the maintenance of the Roman *ethos*, and their identification of themselves with the State of which they were the governors and guardians, imposed limitations on the poets' freedom, and faced them with problems hardly less great than that of amusing the people. We need not then be surprised that the atmosphere was uncongenial to poetry, and that the Roman education with its emphasis on the practical, the growing materialism of the age and the lack of a Roman literature all conspired with the aristocrats' conception of their own duty to prevent the growth of any such poetry as the changed conditions of the first century BC made possible. And as with poetry, so with prose. That same outlook which forbade the nobles to become poets compelled them to turn historian, and since the exigencies of their position did not compel them to set their pens to any other form of prose composition, history remained their one from of literary production. Throughout the nobles are the dominant factor, and if the literature of this period is restricted in scope and somewhat uninspired in content, the blame rests with them.

We may now return to the Lives of Plutarch, with which we began. The reason for that statuesque quality which we note in the Lives of this period is not far to seek; the intimate anecdotes and the motivation which would have enlivened these Lives as they do others are almost wholly absent, because the aristocratic ideal was strongly opposed to such matters being made public, and the nobles successfully prevented any attempt to bruit them abroad. How they dealt with Naevius we have seen, and there was no need to repeat the lesson. The very occasional glimpses of less pleasant aspects, such as the story of Lucius Flamininus and the Gaul, serve to illustrate the point by their exceptional nature. We know of this affair only because Cato – the *novus homo* – when as censor he expelled L. Flamininus from the Senate, made a speech explaining his reasons for this action. The affair could not therefore be concealed. But there must have been equally unpleasant incidents in many a noble's life, of which we know nothing. As for motivation, Plutarch's task was impossible, when his only sources were histories and biographies through whose pages the subjects strode with all the majesty of beings not cursed with human frailties. Only from the historians could some sort of motivation come – such as we have at the end of the *Fabius*. Such motivation does from time to time break in, because the historians with their family differences would have allowed the intrusion of so much. But more than that we are not vouchsafed.

By the end of our period the situation had changed. The moral decline of the aristocracy, which had begun as the exceptional behaviour of a few individuals in Cato's earlier days, had become by now fairly general. The absolute power which as magistrates they exercised in Italy and the provinces, the increased opportunities for the acquisition of wealth from the provinces, and the freedom from foreign danger which might have recalled them to their higher purposes, all conspired to corrupt the high ideals with which they had begun the century. The inefficient conduct of the Spanish war was a sign of the Senatorial inability to manage properly the affairs of State, for which the only solution proved to be the irregular election of Scipio to the command. The better nobles were aware of this, but they were ineffectual to cure.

Polybius could see the trend of things. Although he had described the Roman constitution as depending on the happy balance between the higher magistrates, the Senate and the people, and had shown the strength that the State derived from this interdependence, yet he was later compelled to admit that even a perfect polity was liable to decay from within. 'When a commonwealth,' he says, 'after warding off many great dangers, has arrived at a high pitch of prosperity and undisputed power, it is evident that, by the lengthened continuance of great wealth within it, the manner of life of its citizens will become more extravagant; and that the rivalry for office, and in other spheres of activity, will become fiercer than it ought to be. And as this state of things goes on more and more, the desire of office and the shame of losing reputation, as well as the ostentation and extravagance of living, will prove the beginning of a deterioration. . . . And the people will demand to have all or far the greatest themselves. And when that comes to pass, the constitution will receive a new name, which sounds better than any other in the world, liberty or democracy; but, in fact, it will become that worst of all governments, mob-rule.'[20] Again, when he speaks of Scipio Aemilianus's early years he says that he was anxious to maintain a character for chastity, and to be superior to the standard observed in that respect among his contemporaries. 'This was a glory,' he continues, 'which was not hard to gain at that period in Rome, owing to the general deterioration of morals. . . . This dissoluteness had as it were burst into flame at this period: in the first place, from the prevalent idea that, owing to the destruction of the Macedonian monarch, universal dominion was now secured them beyond dispute; and in the second place, from the immense difference made, both in public and private wealth and splendour, by the importation of the riches of Macedonia into Rome.'[21] It had become clear to him that the ideal State was ceasing to be, and that the fault lay with the nobles themselves, who, corrupted by unchallenged power and wealth, were falling away from their own ideals.

Scipio, too, could see the trend, not without concern; Lucilius's attacks on the defaulting nobles represent Scipio's feelings towards the traitors to the ideal. He attacks their gluttony and luxury at table,[22] holds up to ridicule those who resented Scipio's firm handling of the Roman army encamped about Numantia, where men idled away their time in hot baths, or spent their leisure with the less desirable acquisitions of the camp, which to their great disgust Scipio expelled;[23] he does not hesitate to refer to the dishonesty of particular persons, or to the failures of incompetent generals;[24] he describes the daily scene in the Forum, where senators and people alike hurry about, concerned only to cheat where they can, to outstrip each other in flattery, to give an appearance of honesty, and to lie in wait as though everyone were everyone else's enemy.[25] He states in unadorned language in what virtue consisted, and we may quote it here: 'Virtue is being able to pay in full a fair price in our business dealings and in the affairs which life brings us; virtue is knowing what each affair has within it for a man; virtue is knowing what is right and useful and honourable for a man and what things are good and again what are bad, what is shameful, useless, dishonourable; virtue is knowing the means and the end of seeking a thing, virtue is being able to pay in full the price from our store; virtue is giving that which in all truth is due to honour, being an enemy and no friend of bad men and manners, and on the other hand being a defender of good men and manners; prizing greatly the latter, wishing them well and being a life-long friend to them; and besides all this, thinking our country's interests to be foremost of all, our parents' next, and then thirdly and lastly our own.'[26] Therein, according to them, lay virtue; but neither Scipio's example nor Lucilius's satire had power to turn men from a mode of behaviour which seemed good because it was profitable.

The Gracchi in literature as in all else mark a turning point. The aristocratic ideal had found its basis and its justification during our period; new influences had been made to refine and rationalize a traditional conception, which would otherwise under the impact of new ideas and customs have seemed inadequate or baseless. Yet, like all political ideals, in the moment of its triumph it lost its flexibility, its power of self-adjustment. The aristocrats' refined conception of *virtus* was not – perhaps could not be – modified to suit the changing conditions. And the profound social and economic changes during our period imperiously required a progressive reinterpretation of their ideals in terms of the new situation which was developing. They proved false to their own code when in their attempts to adjust their incomes to new needs and to find an outlet for their newly won capital, by their ruinous agrarian policy they destroyed their own peasants and filled the countryside with slaves. And then by leaving the new economic conditions to be exploited largely by men not of their ranks they allowed the growth of a class whose wealth and influence in time came near to equalling their own, but who, while not imbued with their ideals, had seen their unscrupulous conduct in the acquisition and management of their estates. The intrusion of this class more and more into the public life of the State contributed to the progressive deterioration of public morality for which the aristocrats by their refusal to apply their own principles to the circumstances of moneyed wealth were in the first place responsible. They remained essentially a landowning aristocracy; Cato's *De Agri Cultura* shows to what extent their ruthless standards of business betrayed their own ideal. There is a Gresham's law of morals; and when the nobles should have been striving to improve the moral code of business, they allowed themselves with the State to risk submersion beneath the brackish waters of their own degraded code of money making. Yet if they could not expand their ideal to include business and commerce, they had no choice; for wealth they must have, from whatever source. More and more they found themselves out of tune with their environment, which their own conquests had changed, and yet knowing it they were powerless; for twenty years and more a social and economic problem had called for their statesmanship; and when in 133 BC it became a crisis which challenged the breadth, the very *humanitas* of their ideals, and gave them a last opportunity to show their worthiness to be Rome's sole governors, they elected miserably to act in their own interests.

The individual had been slowly breaking his bonds throughout our period, but until the Gracchi the code of honour among the nobles and prevented any breakaway by the individual in opposition to the opinion of the majority. There had been an uneasy moment when Laelius made his tentative suggestons for reform; but true to the ideal he had withdrawn his project rather than split the nobles. The Gracchi did not withdraw. But the desertion of the Gracchi was not the cause of the nobles' downfall; it was a symptom of their inadequacy. And their continued failure to adapt themselves to new conditions resulted in the Gracchi being the first only of the great individualists.

Their code was no longer obeyed even by their own members; they were exclusive merely, claiming the right to govern without showing their worthiness to do so. The Gracchi and their successors down to Caesar took the first place in Rome; history concerned itself with them. Politics became personal, biographies and autobiographies began to be written. By the time of Sulla a law of libel was necessary, but still the pamphlets came. The age of individualism released the floodgates of individual literature; no aristocracy could impose its limitations; and with the increasing class of educated persons and the gradual multiplicaton of books there grew a Latin literature which was to culminate in the glories of the Augustan age. A civilization that was only dimly aware of the effect of social and economic conditions on men's lives attributed correspondingly more to the individual, and hence all eyes were turned on the men that moulded and seemed to create events. It is not an accident that Plutarch's Lives of the Gracchi have all the elements we found lacking in the earlier *Lives*; the Gracchi are the first to live and move like men, the first of these Romans we feel we know and can understand.

1. 30.23.8ff. The translation is Shuckburgh's.
2. *CIL* I, 2, no. 9. Professor Stuart's translation in 'Epochs of Greek and Roman Biography.'
3. *CIL* I, 2, no. 7. Professor Stuart's translation.
4. *CIL* I, 2, no. 10. Professor Stuart's translation.
5. *CIL* I, 2, no. 11.
6. *CIL* I, 2, no. 15.
7. Pliny, *Nat. Hist.* 7.43.139.
8. Fr. 271 in *Remains of Old Latin*, I, edited by Warmington (Loeb).
9. Fr. 209.
10. Fr. 470.
11. Fr. 467.
12. *CIL* I, 2, no. 1603. Warmington's translation in *Remains of*

Old Latin, IV.

13. *Cato*, 22.2. Perrin's translation in Loeb series.

14. See, for instance, Polybius' description of Aemilius Paullus and Scipio Aemilianus at 18.35.4ff. and 31.25ff.

15. Cato (Jordan), *Carm. Mor.* 2.

16. *De Gram.* 2.

17. Gell. 7.8.5.

18. Warmington's translation, in *op.cit.*, II 139.

19. Don. *ad* Ter. *Eun.* 57.

20. 6.57.5ff. Shuckburgh's translation.

21. 31.25.3ff. Shuckburgh's translation.

22. In Warmington, *Remains of Old Latin*, III, ll. 200-10; 465-6.

23. *Ibid.* ll. 429-31.

24. *Ibid.* ll. 440-2; 499-500.

25. *Ibid.* ll. 1145-51.

26. *Ibid.* ll. 1196-1208.